Formative Assessment in the Secondary Classroom

Formative
Assessment
in the Secondary Classroom

Shirley Clarke

Consultant: Sally Fisher

Hodder Murray

A MEMBER OF THE HODDER HEADLINE GROUP

Orders: please contact Bookpoint Ltd, 130 Milton Park, Abingdon, Oxon OX14 4SB.
Telephone: (44) 01235 827720. Fax: (44) 01235 400454. Lines are open from 9.00 to 6.00,
Monday to Saturday, with a 24-hour message answering service. You can also order
through our website www.hoddereducation.co.uk.

British Library Cataloguing in Publication Data
A catalogue record for this title is available from the British Library

ISBN 0 340 88766 4

First published 2005
Impression number   10 9 8 7 6 5 4 3 2 1
Year   2011 2010 2009 2008 2007 2006 2005

Hodder Headline's policy is to use papers that are natural, renewable and recyclable
products and made from wood grown in sustainable forests. The logging and
manufacturing processes are expected to conform to the environmental regulations of the
country of origin.

Cover photo of students from Welling Secondary School, Bexley, by Jackie Dowse.

Typeset by Servis Filmsetting Ltd, Longsight, Manchester, M13 0LN

Printed in Great Britain for Hodder Murray, a division of Hodder Headline,
338 Euston Road, London NW1 3BH, by Martins the Printers, Berwick-on-Tweed,
Northumberland, TD15 1RS.

Acknowledgements

I would like to thank the following schools and local education authorities for their invaluable contributions to this book:

Upbury Arts College, Medway
The Hundred of Hoo School, Medway
Halyard High School, Luton
Golden Hillock School, Birmingham, especially Pete Weir
Sue Greenfield, Walderslade Girls School, Medway
Carolyn Lyndsay, St Elizabeth School, Tower Hamlets
Phillipa Rouet, Withywood Community School, Bristol
Kevin Brown, Onslow St.Audrey's, Hatfield
Di Pardoe, Bristol EAZ :Success@
Carol Sullivan, Brighton and Hove LEA
Martin Clark, Suffolk LEA
Shaun Knight, Manchester LEA
David Bartlett (Birmingham) and Elizabeth Johnstone (Hereford and Worcester), for the BASS *Assessment for Learning* video
Simon Butler, Devon KS3 foundation subjects advisor
Andrew Noon, Hertfordshire KS3 science consultant
Archie Conway, Luton KS3 science advisor
OFSTED, for writing *Good Assessment in Secondary Schools*: a brilliant resource.
The Kings/Medway/Oxford Formative Assessment Project (KMOFAP) for quotes from teachers
All the teachers who have been part of the amazing UK Learning Teams throughout the last two years
All the students who have inspired me and other researchers with their formative assessment action research.

Special thanks to:

John, Bob and Mike for supporting the writing of this book in every way: food, coffee, housework, love and peace!
Sally Fisher, education consultant: my gratitude for your guidance about the secondary context of this book – and your invaluable additions;

Paul Spenceley and Dave Tuffin from the Hundred of Hoo School for excellent contributions to the book;

Gina D'Auria and Phillipa Rouet, Withywood Community School, Bristol, for equally excellent accounts of their formative assessment practice;

Chas Knight for his patience in dealing with shifting delivery dates and, of course, for being such a superb editor.

Shirley Clarke

Contacts:

www.shirleyclarke-education.org – for information about various courses and for updates on Learning Team findings;
shirleyclarke@wi.rr.com – for direct contact with Shirley.

Contents

Introduction

' *Formative assessment is the process used by teachers and children to recognise and respond to pupil learning, in order to enhance that learning during the activity or task.* '

(Cowie and Bell, 1999)

Formative Assessment, or 'Assessment for Learning', as it has become known, has always existed, sometimes carried out automatically and instinctively by unknowing teachers. Today, it has a respected high profile in UK schools and continues to be developed and explored by educators across all subjects and phases. Rather than being just another government initiative, formative assessment is about teachers being action researchers, taking a few research principles and experimenting with ways of putting them into action. Teachers are continually redefining these strategies, which evolve and develop over time.

As formative assessment has gained such a high profile, in the UK especially, there are inevitable instances of it being misinterpreted. Formative assessment is often seen as using a variety of strategies to ascertain current knowledge and understanding in order to then set targets for improvement, as if the finding out and knowing what needs to be learned next is, in itself, formative. Although these actions are necessary, formative assessment happens *after* the finding out has taken place. It describes the complex process of furthering pupil learning during the learning process, enabling the targets to be met or the quality learning to happen.

In the early days of the National Curriculum, and still today, formative assessment was often defined, wrongly, as simply ongoing summative assessment. The following lists summarise the realities of summative and formative practices in secondary schools at this time.

Summative assessment (measuring attainment)

Current practice for summative assessment tends to consist of the following:

- statutory Key Stage 3 tests
- non-statutory 'optional' tests
- external exams
- commercially produced tests, if chosen by the school
- school and class tests created by teachers
- deciding Key Stage 3 Teacher Assessment levels
- deciding grades: for one piece of work, the end of a unit, a term or a year
- entrance exams for colleges or universities
- recall questions which establish current knowledge or understanding
- any assessment method which aims to establish whether learning has taken place or a target has been met
- any other data about student performance in the school.

Formative assessment (enabling achievement)

Practice drawn from the research base tends to consist of the following:

- clarifying learning objectives and success criteria at the planning stage, as a framework for formative assessment processes *(Chapter 1)*;
- sharing learning objectives and success criteria with students, both long term and for individual lessons *(Chapter 2)*;

- appropriate and effective questioning which develops the learning rather than attempts to measure it *(Chapter 3)*;

- focusing oral and written feedback, whether from teacher or student, around the development of learning objectives and meeting of targets *(Chapter 5)*;

- organising targets so that students' achievement is based on previous achievement as well as aiming for the next step (ipsative referencing) *(Chapter 5)*;

- involving students in self- and peer evaluation *(Chapter 6)*;

- raising students' self-efficacy and holding a belief that all students have the potential to learn and to achieve (*throughout the book*).

The current context for secondary schools

The National Curriculum, statutory testing and external tests and league tables present the same opportunities, pressures and problems for both primary and secondary schools. The secondary context is the focus of this book, so the following issues are acknowledged:

- The pressures of meeting departmental/school targets/performance management targets for external examinations (SATs/GCSE) has made many teachers wary of trying something different.

- Subject coverage still dominates and many teachers see formative assessment as something else to be fitted in.

   This has been the case for some primary teachers, but the high profile of formative assessment has encouraged teachers to look at what it really means. Doing formative assessment is about changing the way in which a lesson is constructed and managed, the culture and ethos of the classroom and the quality of questioning and feedback. Most of all, it is about the involvement of students in the learning process, beyond anything traditional teaching has previously allowed. The proven effect of teaching in this way is that students do BETTER at tests than before and become life-long independent learners.

■ Since Curriculum 2000, there is more flexibility, but the legacy of pressure to achieve coverage has left many teachers wary of using their professional judgment.

Many teachers knowingly sacrifice understanding for coverage. The 2004 OFSTED framework has one key focus: the achievement of students in relation to intended learning. Coverage and accountability have taken a back seat in pursuit of this ultimate evidence of effective teaching and learning.

■ Staff turnover is often high, so there is a constant need to train new staff with no extra time available.

An agreed formative assessment policy needs to define the principles and practice within the school. One or two days of shadowing another teacher seems to be the most effective way of helping a new teacher take on formative assessment.

■ It is difficult to keep one focus high on the whole school agenda, and difficult to create time to reflect. But if formative assessment is put on the back burner, impetus and enthusiasm wane.

Once teachers really get going with formative assessment, they find the impact on student learning is so great, they can't go back to what they were doing before. However, it needs a 'champion' in a school for the first few years to keep it high profile.

■ It is difficult to monitor formative assessment across a large school and difficult to create meeting times to share good practice and ideas.

See Chapter 7.

■ Many schools' assessment policies appear at odds with formative assessment and this is confusing for staff. For instance, many schools now use tracking systems where numbers for effort/attainment/homework, etc, are recorded and sent out to parents.

■ Teachers often do not have continuity in terms of the classes they teach. Every September they are often given an entirely different set of groups. These groups may have had very differing experiences of formative assessment, depending on who previously taught them.

The whole school, therefore, has to be committed to formative assessment and develop an ethos in which it is respected and given high profile. The key supporter must be the head.

The history of formative assessment in the UK

By 1997, the assessment emphasis from Government in England was quite clearly focused on **summative** assessment. Even Teacher Assessment was described as the end-of-key-stage levelling process, rather than the ongoing understanding of students' understanding. A group of assessment academics, naming themselves the Assessment Reform Group, decided that something significant needed to happen to convince policymakers to change their emphasis, or even just to acknowledge the power of **formative** rather than summative assessment.

To that end, Paul Black and Dylan Wiliam, from King's College, University of London, were commissioned to find out whether or not formative assessment could be shown to raise levels of attainment. The pair embarked on a year's work, trawling through all the studies since 1988 which involved aspects such as sharing learning goals, student self-evaluation and feedback. Many studies were rejected through lack of rigour, as Black and Wiliam decided to take account only of those where a control group had been set up and students had been tested before and after the trial, so that learning gains could be measured and compared.

They found that formative assessment strategies do indeed raise standards of attainment, with a greater effect for students of lower achievement. At GCSE they were able to calculate that the improvement amounts to an increase of between one and two grades.

The resulting lengthy article was published (Black and Wiliam, 1998), and received national and international interest over the findings. Black and Wiliam produced a digest of the article, entitled *Inside the Black Box*, which summarised the key findings. This was followed by *Assessment for Learning: Beyond the Black Box*, written by the Assessment Reform Group (1999).

The purpose of these books was to begin to bullet-point the conditions for success in the classroom, making them more accessible to teachers. Both digests give schools ideal material to use for parent communication and in policies, as they consist of many summary statements. My own work with teachers, including various research projects and formats for action research, aims to flesh out and define in more practical terms what formative assessment actually looks like in the classroom.

Bringing together so many studies led to the identification of clear themes. However, one theme emerged which Black and Wiliam saw as the key to successful learning: the importance of **high self-efficacy**. Self-efficacy describes how you feel about your various abilities, as opposed to how you feel about your inner self (self-esteem). Because of its centrality, the ways in which students' self-efficacy can be raised or lowered is dealt with throughout this book.

The key findings from Black and Wiliam's research (Assessment Reform Group, 1999) are reproduced here:

' *The research indicates that improving learning through assessment depends on five, deceptively simple, key factors:*

■ *the provision of effective feedback to students;*

■ *the active involvement of students in their own learning;*

■ *adjusting teaching to take account of the results of assessment;*

■ *a recognition of the profound influence assessment has on the motivation and self-esteem of students, both of which are crucial influences on learning;*

■ *the need for students to be able to assess themselves and understand how to improve.* '

(page 4)

This was further broken down to include:

' ■ *sharing learning goals with students;*

■ *involving students in self-assessment;*

■ *providing feedback which leads to students recognising their next steps and how to take them;*

■ *underpinned by confidence that every student can improve.* '

(page 7)

The inhibiting factors identified included:

■ *a tendency for teachers to assess quantity of work and presentation rather than the quality of learning;*

■ *greater attention given to marking and grading, much of it tending to lower the self-esteem of students, rather than to provide advice for improvement;*

■ *a strong emphasis on comparing students with each other which demoralises the less successful learners;*

■ *teachers' feedback to students often serves managerial and social purposes rather than helping them to learn more effectively*

(page 5)

An invaluable OFSTED publication, *Good Assessment in Secondary Schools* (2003), includes a list of the features seen in classrooms where formative assessment was deemed to be successful:

■ A welcome to the students, who were personally valued and knew that they would be expected and helped to do their best.

■ Clarity of aims and expected outcomes, discussed at the outset.

■ A range of methods that give students some responsibility for organising how they learn, and that involve them in a variety of ways – through presentations, displays, using the whiteboard, simulations, role play, quizzes, modelling, the use of memory and recall techniques, and through reflecting on the value of what has been achieved.

■ A collaborative approach to learning, with a strong emphasis on analysis and discussion.

■ Opportunities for divergent thinking in an atmosphere that ensures students do not feel bad if they make a mistake.

The publication also includes many cameo descriptions of lessons, some of which are reproduced in this book, and practices that help to bring key principles to life.

Priorities

In order for formative assessment to be embedded in practice, it is vital that teachers have *students' learning* as their priority: not their teaching or the opinions of outside parties. This is easy to say, but less easy to implement. This book takes account of the realities of the classroom and external pressures, within the context of striving for a whole-school rationale. Ways of facilitating and nurturing students' learning and their desire to learn must override all other aims. Teaching is, of course, a key instrument, and throughout the book strategies are shared and analysed so that the best of practice can 'travel'.

Formative assessment is a powerful vehicle for focusing on effective learning. However, it is not a quick fix: it takes time, thought and discussion to become embedded. It also involves, in many cases, a gradual power shift, through modelling and training, enabling students to gradually take more and more control over their learning and the decisions they make to enhance that learning.

Askew and Lodge's (2000) framework for feedback encapsulates the entire learning journey, from teachers' control to student power.

Learning style	View of feedback
Instruction *(direct teaching)*	The Gift
Construction *(dialogue between teacher and student)*	Ping-pong
Co-construction *(free-flow dialogue between teachers and students separately and together)*	Loops

(Askew and Lodge, 2000)

We are aiming for 'loops', but we may need to include more 'gifts' and 'ping-pong' at the beginning of the continuum of control in order to reach that point.

The same principles and continuum apply when working with adults in their professional development. For some teachers, introducing formative assessment will require a re-evaluation of how they teach and how they perceive that students learn. Formative assessment only works when teachers come to own it for themselves – when they can talk to others about the way it works in their classroom, and when they become part of the huge number of teachers continually discovering and understanding better ways of helping students not only to learn but to love learning.

1 Creating a learning culture in which formative assess- ment can exist

> ❝ *If students don't learn the way we teach . . . perhaps we should teach the way they learn.* ❞
>
> *(Eppig, 1981)*

> ❝ *Every teacher who wants to practise formative assessment must reconstruct the teaching contracts so as to counteract the habits acquired by their students.* ❞
>
> *(Perrenoud, 1991)*

In order for formative assessment to take place, we need to be clear about our aims for students' learning – not just *what* we want them to learn, but *how* we want them to learn, so that they leave school with the desire to learn and with enough knowledge about how to do this if left to their own devices. This, of course, means we also have to look at how we are teaching.

The search for answers about how learners learn and how teachers need to teach is never-ending, and the main source of answers is teachers' own findings. The following section outlines the most significant theories about learning and teaching to which we need to pay attention when considering formative assessment and effective feedback.

The constructivist classroom

Formative assessment is often linked with the **constructivist** model, in which the *learner* is responsible for the learning and the construction of knowledge, through cooperative situations, open-ended questioning, discussion and meaningful contexts.

 The most important single factor influencing learning is what the learner already knows. Ascertain this and teach him accordingly.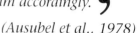

(Ausubel et al., 1978)

Although it would seem obvious that teachers should create learning environments which follow Ausubel's wisdom, some teachers resist the constructivist approach – because they are embedded in their old way of teaching, they don't believe it will make students learn better, they are satisfied with their students' grades and want no more for them, or they are worried that they will somehow lose control if students are given more stake in their learning. For some teachers, particularly where behavioural problems are perceived, this is a very real worry. How will students be drawn back if the 'reins' are loosened? How will 'authority' be maintained and student behaviour managed within this new teacher–student relationship?

The constructivist classroom involves the teacher in taking risks and systematically relinquishing control. Ironically, though, rather than losing control, the teacher gains more satisfaction and finds him or herself in a classroom in which students are more motivated to learn. Once students understand their true place as learners, with the teacher as a facilitator, they let go of the struggle to conform to the teacher's wishes and do what he or she wants them to do and focus instead on finding the best ways of learning. In these circumstances, they expect the teacher and others to help them learn.

The characteristics of a constructivist classroom inevitably include the use of formative assessment. Brooks and Brooks (1993) list twelve descriptors of constructivist teaching behaviours, which should be helpful in clarifying the constructivist approach. I provide some interpretation in italics.

1   Constructivist teachers encourage and accept student autonomy and initiative – *students frame their own questions and find answers.*

2   Constructivist teachers use raw data and primary sources, along with manipulative, interactive and physical materials – *students look for evidence rather than receiving knowledge passively and link concepts to real-life situations, events and objects.*

3   When framing tasks, constructivist teachers use cognitive terminology such as 'classify', 'analyse', 'predict' and 'create' – *teachers go beyond literal questions of how, what and who, thus encouraging higher-level thinking.*

4   Constructivist teachers allow student responses to drive lessons, shift instructional strategies and alter content – *the curriculum and exam syllabi determine what must be taught, not how . . . whether the learning objective is being met or not is the prime concern – lesson content should change to best facilitate student learning.*

5   Constructivist teachers inquire about students' understandings of concepts before sharing their own understanding of these concepts – *concept mapping or brainstorming before unit planning takes place, or at beginnings of lessons, ensures that the teacher takes account of students' current understandings and interests.*

6   Constructivist teachers encourage students to engage in dialogue, both with the teacher and with one another – *students are encouraged to present their own ideas as well as being permitted to hear and reflect on the ideas of others; paired two-minute discussions before general feedback leads to more powerful construction of new understandings or reflection of old ones.*

7   Constructivist teachers encourage student enquiry by asking thoughtful, open-ended questions and encouraging students to ask questions of each other – *teachers use a range of questioning strategies to ensure maximum involvement, thinking and articulation*

8   Constructivist teachers seek elaboration of students' initial responses – *by using a multiple-choice approach: 'What exactly do you mean? Do you mean this . . ., do you mean that . . ., or do you have an idea of your own?' and delving. Modelling possible student responses gives students a way in: 'I think your answer to this might be . . . or . . . What do you think?.'*

9   Constructivist teachers engage students in experiences that might engender contradictions to their initial hypotheses and then encourage discussion – *teachers ask questions which set up contradictions to encourage discussion: e.g. 'So it is wrong to steal. But would it still be wrong to rob a bank if your children were starving?'*

10 Constructivist teachers allow 'wait time' after posing questions – *students need approximately five seconds after the question is asked – experimenting with 'no hands up' and talking partners, so all have a chance of being asked and the negative comparison effect is avoided.*

11   Constructivist teachers provide time for students to construct relationships and create metaphors – *asking 'what if?' questions to encourage links between ideas and giving students time to create metaphors for their understandings.*

12   Constructivist teachers nurture students' natural curiosity through frequent use of the learning cycle model – (*i*) *students interact with selected materials and generate questions and hypotheses; (ii) teacher focuses student's questions as a way of introducing the concept; (iii) students work on new problems as a way of applying the concept.*

Multiple intelligences

Howard Gardner (1983) introduced the idea, based on research about different abilities being located in different parts of the brain, that we have several different types of intelligences:

- linguistic intelligence
- logical or mathematical intelligence
- musical intelligence
- spatial and visual intelligence
- kinaesthetic intelligence
- interpersonal intelligence
- intrapersonal intelligence

Some people argue that there are other types of intelligence missed from this list, such as *commonsense intelligence, naturalist intelligence* (the ability to work with nature) and *emotional intelligence.*

The implications of these ideas are that we need to be considering students' preferred learning styles, motivations and natural tendencies, and that each person has a range of abilities which should be nourished and expressed throughout their education.

We need to structure learning in ways which are compatible with the way the brain learns naturally:

- *when it is trying to make sense;*
- *when it is building on what it already knows;*
- *when it recognises the significance of what it is doing;*
- *when it is working in complex, multiple perspectives;*
- *when it is learning collaboratively in a social/team setting.*

(Abbott, 1994)

The intelligences do not operate in isolation for any of us, nor do they develop at the same rate. Many students (and adults) believe that they lack cognitive ability in any subject at which they are slower than their peers. For some aspects of their learning, people often need more time, input and especially effort to be applied.

Learning occurs when new links are formed between neurons in the cortex of the brain. These links form when we have to think, and the more thinking, the more secure the links become. Perkins (1992) believes that the traditional way of schooling is 'back to front':

❛*The rationale can be boiled down to a single sentence: Learning is a consequence of thinking. Retention, understanding and the active use of knowledge can be brought about by learning experiences in which learners think about and think with what they are learning. . . . The conventional pattern says that, first, students acquire knowledge. Only then do they think with and about the knowledge that they have absorbed. Far from thinking coming after knowledge, knowledge comes on the coattails of thinking. As we think about and with the content that we are learning, we truly learn it. . . .* ❜

(Perkins, 1992)

Some important lessons from Japan

The Japanese culture emphasises the importance of *effort*. This focuses students on learning rather than competition and performance. Students receive as many congratulations for effort and perseverance, even if the final outcome is a failure, as for academic achievement. They stay motivated for long periods of time because they know everyone believes the learning is possible for them, although it may take some time and effort.

Two books which have inspired me most in recent years are *The Learning Gap* (Stevenson and Stigler, 1992) and *The Teaching Gap* (Stigler and Hiebert, 1999). They compare American classrooms with Japanese classrooms and examine both cultures in depth. Thousands of hours of video were studied to come up with the findings. Some of the stark differences reported between US and Japanese methods, bearing in mind that lessons were generalised, are relevant for the UK classroom and other Western settings. I am not recommending the entire Japanese education system, simply highlighting those aspects which are relevant and useful for ours. My main point here is how the Japanese model promotes a high level of motivation, both for students and teachers, because there is a different way of seeing the role of the educator and the student as a learner compared to the traditional Western view. Some examples of the differences are given in Fig. 1.1.

The team also discovered many cultural differences that are impossible to replicate, like parental attitude to education (e.g. in Japan even the poorest homes have a desk for each student, whereas in American homes the adults' needs take priority). The parallels with the UK classroom are clear. We cannot simply tweak the existing culture in order to make learning the priority: we have to create institutions which have different ways of valuing learning.

The social context of learning

We need to think not only about the learning, but the situation in which the learning takes place and the influence of those factors in promoting or demoting motivation and effective learning.

Vygotsky (1978) established the *zone of proximal development* as the challenge factor in learning – the difference between what students can do independently and what they can accomplish with the support of others. The constructivist model promotes cooperative situations as essential for effective learning, with much classroom talk – between students and teachers and between students together.

It is through group discussions and cooperative learning situations that trust develops, which in itself motivates and makes secure the learning context for the student. As Abrami et al. (1995) say: *'Co-operation promotes trust, trust promotes co-operation, greater co-operation results in greater trust.'*

Fig. 1.1

US lessons	Japanese lessons
US teachers see mixed-ability groupings as a problem.	Japanese teachers see mixed ability as a gift: individual differences are seen as beneficial for the class because they produce a range of ideas, methods and solutions that provide the material for students' discussion and reflection.
US teachers differentiate by ability.	Japanese teachers see this as unfairly limiting and as prejudging what students are capable of learning: all students should have the opportunity to learn the same material.
US teachers hold students' attention by increasing pace, by praising work and behaviour, by having real-life tasks and by their own enthusiasm, humour and 'coolness'.	Japanese teachers believe that the learning itself is the greatest motivational tool.
US teachers tend to use an overhead projector or computer for teaching points, turning it off when they want students to listen or work – they see it as an attention and motivational tool.	Japanese teachers use a chalkboard/whiteboard as a continuous record of a lesson, to which students have constant access.
US students sit for many hours without a break.	School days are longer but each lesson is followed by a short playground break.
Most US lessons are continually interrupted.	Japanese lessons are never interrupted – the lesson is seen as sacrosanct.

The popular Critical Skills Program advocates developing a 'Full Value Contract' with students to underpin the vision of a collaborative learning classroom. Weatherley (2000) suggests leading to this by organising a carousel brainstorming session (with rules of brainstorming, such as not judging or criticising people's ideas) around key questions. The following questions, produced by one teacher, used a sporting analogy of the importance of drawing on the different strengths of the team:

■ *What will our classroom look like and sound like if we all play hard?*

■ *What will our classroom look like and sound like if we all play safe physically?*

■ *What will our classroom look like and sound like if we all play safe emotionally?*

■ *What will our classroom look like and sound like if we all play fair?*

Students move around these four questions, adding to each other's responses, ticking those they agree with and adding their own suggestions. The finished product, once abbreviated, is displayed whenever the class is working with that particular teacher.

Some extracts (8 points from 18) from the Full Value Contract produced by one secondary class are given in Fig. 1.2.

Motivation and self-esteem

How students perceive themselves and their ability is central to the success of the learning environment. Unless we pay attention to the factors that increase or decrease students' self-esteem and motivation, we are often working fruitlessly.

The recognised vital ingredients of self-esteem (Youngs, in Dryden and Vos, 2001) are:

■ physical safety (*freedom from physical harm*)

■ emotional safety (*the absence of intimidation and fears*)

■ identity (*I am proud of being who I am*)

Fig. 1.2 Extracts from a Full Value Contract

'As a full and responsible member of this learning community, I agree to:

1. Respect the privacy of other group members. . . .

3. Ask for what I want and need, but not expect to get everything that I want.

4. Speak only for myself and not others. . . .

6. Express my feelings in a way that shows respect for myself   and for others. . . .

9. Decide on if or how I want to be different as a result of my experience in this community and develop a plan for changing. . . .

10. Be willing to receive and to give open and honest feedback. . . .

16. Seek quality in both individual and collaborative work and in my interaction with others.

17. Maintain a sense of humour. . . .'

(Weatherley, 2000)

- affiliation (*a sense of belonging*)
- competence (*I can do this to the best of my ability*)
- mission (*my life has meaning and direction*).

Identity and Competence are also known as *self-worth* and *self-efficacy,* respectively. People often have a high sense of self-worth yet a low sense of self-efficacy (*I'm a nice person but I'm no good at anything*), or vice-versa (*I'm quite clever but people don't really like me*). Students' self-worth is developed mainly within their home and social situation, whereas their sense of self-efficacy can be greatly influenced by their educational experiences.

Many schools lead students to believe that it is ability that leads to success, rather than effort. Students believe that their ability for each subject is something that cannot be changed. Various researchers (e.g. Vispoel and Austin, 1995) urge teachers to talk to students about the nature of learning: that learning is a continuum on which we are all placed and that, *given enough time and input*, anyone can master.

A driving test is the perfect example: why do English people put themselves through the extreme stress of a second driving test after failing the first? Because, of course, they are highly motivated to drive. But something more important is happening. Can you imagine, on returning to your family after failing the test, being told to forget about driving, as you are clearly finding it too hard, just as many other members of the family have in the past? The idea is ludicrous. Our families, of course, assume we will be repeating the test and, in the meantime, having more lessons. Regardless of ability or background, there is a deep-rooted belief in our culture, that, given enough time and input, everyone can reach this recognised standard. Imagine if this belief could be transferred to school subjects! However, teachers have to truly *believe* it of their students for their potential to be fully realised.

There are many ways in which the traditions of the classroom set up a comparison effect, where students believe that, compared to others in the class, they lack ability. If this perception continues within a subject, the outcome is inevitable: the student loses motivation and avoids investing effort in the subject, usually opting out at some stage. The most explicit ways in which we set up the comparison effect are by grading every piece of work (see Chapter 4) and by giving external rewards (e.g. merit marks, house points), where at the end of a lesson, only certain students will receive these things, even though all have achieved something against the success criteria of the lesson. This is not to be confused with qualification certificates of various kinds, which all students have an equal chance of gaining over time.

External rewards can impact in various ways:

■ They encourage students to strive for the reward rather than the achievement.

■ They conflict with investigation and deep thinking, because we take the quickest route to get the reward.

■ They encourage students to be competitive rather than cooperative.

■ Teachers claim that they give external rewards fairly and for a range of good work and deeds, but in various studies where external rewards have been tracked, it always emerges that three groups of students receive them the most: *students with special needs, brighter students* and *disruptive students* (when they are not!). Ignored every time are the average, self-contained students who work solidly and cause no behavioural problems.

■ They result in only short-term motivational gains.

The most important point here, of course, is to decide whether you want a performance or a learning ethos. Do we really want students to believe that the most significant educational achievement in the school is to be given a merit mark? Formative assessment is 'ipsative': students are competing against themselves, not others. All students should be able to achieve some success against the success criteria in any lesson, so the notion of awarding a few rewards to particular students sets up the comparison effect over and over again.

Teachers sometimes argue that the real world is full of external rewards and students should be prepared for this. Yet students will be more confident and more able to tackle those situations if they have been allowed to develop their abilities *without* continual reminders that they are not as able as their peers. Many schools remove external rewards in favour of verbal celebrations of achievement and an ethos of high expectation and a 'can do' culture. Students, far from being distressed, tend not to notice their removal, and many are relieved.

Some other ways in which the comparison effect is set up:

■ Body language, tone of voice and phrasing in the classroom when interacting with individuals: these are powerful 'give-aways' to students about how the teacher perceives.

■ The use of classroom assistants in the classroom: do they automatically sit with the same students, before the task instructions have taken place, giving a clear message that the student will be unable to do the work without help?

■ Setting: many students are, cognitively, placed in the wrong set, although they present themselves in a way which makes them appear to be in the right set, mainly by their attitude – usually a direct result of their self-efficacy.

■ The way in which students perceive difficulty as failure, because of a sympathetic approach: challenge is an exciting indication of new learning and needs to be communicated as such (*'I'm pleased that this is making you think. It means you are learning something new. If you already knew how to do it, there would be no new learning.'*). Responses like this allow students to see their true place in the classroom – as the client needing to learn. The comparison effect is relieved and students more readily seek help, from each other and from teachers.

Carol Dweck's (1986) work on motivation summarises what happens if you get students to focus on competitive structures (*performance orientation*) rather than on what they have learnt and what they need to do to improve (*learning orientation*) – Fig. 1.3.

Fig. 1.3

Performance orientation (*I want the best grade/merit mark/ to be first*)	Learning orientation (*I want to work hard/I want to learn and know how to improve*)
Belief that ability leads to success.	Belief that effort leads to success.
Concern to be judged as able and to perform.	Belief in one's ability to improve and learn.
Satisfaction from doing better than others or succeeding with little effort.	Preference for challenging tasks.
Emphasis on interpersonal competition and public evaluation.	Derives satisfaction from personal success at difficult tasks.
Helplessness: evaluates self negatively when task is difficult.	Applies problem solving and self-instructions when engaged in tasks.

Finally, this quotation from *Inside the Black Box* summarises findings about the importance of the teacher's role in raising students' self-esteem:

Where the classroom culture focuses on rewards, "gold stars", grades or place-in-the-class ranking, then students look for the ways to obtain the best marks rather than at the needs of their learning. The reported consequence is that where they have any choice, students avoid difficult tasks. They also spend time and energy looking for the "right answer". Many are reluctant to ask questions out of fear of failure. Students who encounter difficulties and poor results are led to believe that they lack ability, and this belief leads them to attribute their difficulties to a defect in themselves about which they cannot do a

great deal. So they "retire hurt", avoid investing effort in learning which could only lead to disappointment, and try to build up their self-esteem in other ways. Whilst the high achievers can do well in such a culture, the overall result is to enhance the frequency and the extent of underachievement. What is needed is a culture of success, backed by a belief that all can achieve. **,**

(Black and Wiliam, 1998)

Conclusions

It is essential that all teachers within a school develop a teaching and learning policy together, to be committed to their beliefs and ideals for their students and their school. Without this, any departure into the world of formative assessment will be fraught with problems. Teachers who do not understand its conceptual framework will pay lip service to the ideas involved in formative assessment, but behind closed doors will carry on with their usual practice. Teachers who do understand, on the other hand, will recognise much of their existing practice already. It is on that practice that we need to build, in order to achieve a universal school learning culture.

Key principles

- Many elements of formative assessment are reflected in constructivist beliefs about learning.

- We need to plan for different intelligences and styles of learning.

- Effort should be applauded as much as achievement.

- Many traditions of Western education lower students' self-efficacy.

- We should focus on a learning orientation rather than a performance orientation.

- The social context plays a powerful part in motivation and the effectiveness of learning.

- Schools need to have a well-discussed and agreed teaching and learning policy to underpin any work on formative assessment: this might result *after* trialling formative assessment!

INSET ideas (departmental or whole-staff meetings)

1. Use the twelve descriptors of constructivist teaching behaviours in a staff meeting, having circulated them in advance. Get teachers in groups to take two or three of the points: discuss and come up with some practical examples. Feed back the examples to each other and have a general discussion about the implications for practice and for any change that might be required.
2. Look at Howard Gardner's descriptions of the different intelligences and discuss in a staff meeting.
   (a) Decide alone and then in pairs on own preferred learning orientations.
   (b) Use short-term plans, schemes of work/lesson plans to analyse a day's lessons: which intelligences do they favour? How can we strike a better balance?
3. Ask teachers to experiment for one week in the classroom, making a big deal about the amount of effort applied, whether the outcome is poor or excellent. In a subsequent staff meeting, feed back the impact on students' attitude to learning and their self-efficacy.
4. Discuss the use of classroom assistants, including them in this discussion, and decide on more flexible patterns.

2 Learning objectives and process success criteria

' A teacher's planning should provide opportunities for both learner and teacher to obtain and use information about progress towards learning goals. It also has to be flexible to respond to initial and emerging ideas and skills. Planning should include strategies to ensure that learners understand the goals they are pursuing and the criteria that will be applied in assessing their work. How learners will receive feedback, how they will take part in assessing their learning and how they will be helped to make further progress should also be planned. '

(Assessment Reform Group, 2002)

Balancing the curriculum

Since the introduction of the National Curriculum there has really only been one way of thinking about learning objectives: in terms of *skills, concepts* and *knowledge*. These are the learning objectives which we have decided students need to learn, either via lessons in school or by simply being alive: the taught specifics. As well as these, it is useful to include 'application' learning objectives, where we bring together many specific aspects into a 'big picture' learning objective.

Fig. 2.1 shows a closer look at the different types of taught specifics, with implications for teaching. Fig. 2.2 gives examples of applications.

Fig. 2.1 Taught specifics (long- or short-term learning objectives, often broken down)

Learning objective category	Examples	Implications for teaching
Closed skills	■ To be able to use speech marks ■ To write a percentage as a fraction in lowest terms	These have right or wrong answers or can only be done in one way. Differentiation by task is usually necessary.
Open skills	■ To draw scientific conclusions ■ To write complex sentences	Result in a continuum of achievement rather than right or wrong answers. Differentiation by outcome is appropriate to ensure maximum achievement for all.
Knowledge	■ To know what longitude and latitude are ■ To know how the Roman army was organised	Long-term learning objectives which need to be broken down for individual lessons. Overfocusing on knowledge rather than the related skills means nothing is left when the knowledge is usually forgotten.
Concepts	■ To understand the causes of river floods ■ To understand the importance of healthy living	Long-term learning objectives which need to be broken down for lessons. Need more investigative learning.

Fig. 2.2 Application learning objectives (the big picture: a test of previously learned or taught specifics)

Test (informal or formal)	■ Write a comprehensive account ■ Design and carry out a scientific experiment ■ Solve problems using Pythagoras's Theorem	Usually takes place *after* teaching, often better *before* so that teaching can build on prior knowledge. Need a balance between taught specifics and applications.

Implications of the taught specifics/applications model

Thinking of learning objectives as taught specifics and applications allows us to clarify some issues. Firstly, *it is impossible to make all learning objectives specific* and explicit: *application* learning objectives are necessarily broad.

Secondly, *it is of little use making ongoing* **summative** *judgements (how many students have understood this?) of the taught specifics,* because they look as if they can do it at the time. The acid test of the taught specifics is in the applications: these are the only valid and reliable contexts for summative decisions. Ongoing assessment for taught specifics is best focused around formative assessment: establishing where success is taking place and reinforcing that, and identifying improvement needs as skills are being developed.

Finally, there are profound implications for the way we should plan over time. It is clear that *we need a balance between the two types of learning objectives,* sometimes with applications taking place **before and after** the specific teaching rather than simply after the teaching.

Reasons for integrating more application learning objectives include:

- You find out what they already know that hasn't yet been taught.

- You find out whether they really know what you have taught – can they apply it in this context?

- It gives students the whole picture, therefore making connections easier and providing purpose, motivation and interest.

- Things go wrong, resulting in students being able to more easily identify the need for the next element to be taught.

- You find out individual students' target needs and sometimes whole-class needs which provide important planning information.

Getting learning objectives right

Muddling the learning objective with the context

The more we learn about formative assessment, the more important it seems to be to ensure that learning objective/s for lessons are appropriate. If learning objectives are unclear, students cannot begin to carry out the required learning effectively. If they have not been told where they are going, it is unlikely that they will arrive. Muddled learning objectives lead to mismatched activities, which may not fulfil the learning objective. They also lead to inappropriate focus and awkward success criteria.

'**To understand the effect of banana production on the banana producers**' is a geography long-term learning objective in which the context has been included. The learning objective should, of course, read:

'To understand the effect of production on the producers.'

Given the first learning objective, it is likely that students will believe that the effect of production on the producers is only an issue about bananas. Their attention and perhaps the teacher's focus is likely to dwell too heavily on details about bananas rather than the real learning objective. By separating the learning objective explicitly from its context, students are able to see the connections: *that learning objectives can often be applied to a number of different contexts*.

Fig. 2.3 gives some examples of learning objectives separated from the context.

If you want the students to learn it, it needs to be part of the learning objective. If it is the *context* for the learning (the 'how' or vehicle), it needs to stay out. It is important to get this right, not only to *ensure appropriate focus* and connections, but also in order to *plan appropriate success criteria*, which need to link directly with the learning objective.

Fig. 2.3

BEFORE . . . Learning objective unclear	AFTER . . . Learning objective	Context
To present an argument for and against abortion.	To present a reasoned argument including 'for' and 'against' positions.	Abortion debate.
To know what the local vicar does.	To know the duties of a religious leader.	The local vicar.
To produce a questionnaire about shopping patterns.	To be able to investigate the distribution of an economic activity.	Interviews with family about where they shop and how their shopping patterns have changed.
To analyse five different diets and decide what would constitute a balanced diet.	To understand the ingredients of and need for a balanced diet.	Analysing different diets.
To create a written description of a friend.	To be able to create an effective characterisation.	Describe a friend.

The power of process success criteria

For some time, many teachers have created *product* success criteria using words like *'By the end, you will have. . .'*. We know that it is important for students to know the final product or outcome expected of a long-term learning objective. However, students also need to have learning objectives broken down for individual lessons and to have *process* success criteria to help them while they are engaged in the task. Process success criteria summarise the key steps or ingredients the student needs in order to fulfil the learning objective – the main things to do, include or focus on. These give a framework for formative assessment to take place. Issues of quality are discussed from page 34.

Some examples of product and process success criteria

Example 1

Long-term learning objective To know that some materials conduct heat at different rates.

PRODUCT success criterion: Be able to explain how different materials conduct heat at different rates.

More helpful:

Broken-down lesson learning objective: To record results accurately and explain patterns using your scientific knowledge.

Context: four metals crucifix heating

PROCESS success criteria:

Remember to –

- record the time taken each time
- compare results (differentiated):
    1. *describe* rates of conduction
    2. *apply* conduction to less familiar situations
    3. *give reasons* for different rates of conduction using particles.

Example 2

Long-term learning objective: To be able to calculate area of different 2D shapes.

PRODUCT success criterion: Use the correct formula in calculating area of different 2D shapes.

More helpful:

Broken-down lesson learning objective: To be able to calculate the area of a triangle.

Context: Worksheet with various triangles.

PROCESS success criteria:

Remember to –

- identify and measure the base and height
- multiply the base by the height and divide by 2
- record in units squared.

Example 3

Lesson learning objective: To write an effective characterisation.

PRODUCT success criterion: Someone who reads it will feel they really know the person.

More helpful:

PROCESS success criteria:

Remember to include at least two of the following -

- the character's hobbies and interest
- the character's attitude to self and others
- examples of the character's extrovert or introvert personality
- examples of the character's likes and dislikes.

N.B. **Closed** skills usually have chronological success criteria. **Open** skills usually have ingredient style success criteria from which, in some instances, students choose (as in the characterisation example above).

Looking back at the 'before and after' table (Fig. 2.3), it is clear that attempting to create success criteria for the muddled learning objectives would be a difficult task. For instance, success criteria for *'To know what the local vicar does'* might have us asking him questions about what he has for breakfast, whereas planning success criteria for *'To know the duties of a religious leader'* will focus us on the appropriate questions.

Process success criteria are usually given to students during or at the end of a lesson as activity instructions, but have on the whole been verbalised only, resulting in many students forgetting the key things to focus on. Spending a few minutes during the lesson or at the end of the lesson gathering these key points from students, writing them on the whiteboard and getting them to write them in their books to accompany their work means they have a vital visual reminder while they are engaged in the task.

The following examples bring learning objectives, contexts and process success criteria together.

English Y7

Learning objective	Context	Process success criteria
Write persuasively using different techniques	Letter to local MP regarding fox hunting	Remember to include: ■ A statement of your viewpoint ■ A number of reasons for this, with evidence ■ A number of reasons from an alternative standpoint ■ Attempts at striking up empathy with the recipient ■ Recommended alternative action ■ A summary ■ Reasoning connectives

Mathematics Y8

Learning objective	Context	Process success criteria
To share a quantity into a ratio	Worksheet	Remember to: ■ Add the parts e.g. 2:3 2+3=5 ■ Write each ratio as a fraction 2/5 : 3/5 ■ Multiply each fraction by the whole e.g. 2/5 of 20

Music KS3

Learning objective	Context	Process success criteria
To understand and explain the use of musical instruments and elements in programmatic music	A chosen story: groups compose programmatic music	Remember to: ■ Create a balanced 3-section composition ■ Use tone, pitch and dynamics to reflect the events and mood of the story ■ Use the instruments creatively

Geography Y10

Learning objective	Context	Process success criteria
To know ways of controlling drought	Savannah grassland	Remember to: ■ List the different causes of drought ■ Explain how these could be reduced ■ List your recommendations for how people can cope and live with drought ■ Make comparisons with 'drought' in the UK

History Y7

Learning objective	Context	Process success criteria
To weigh up the advantages and disadvantages of different types of Roman government	Summarising text and creating timeline of government changes and key events + discussion and analysis, then presenting own conclusion in pairs	Remember to: ■ Describe each type of government ■ Consider some of the pros and cons of each ■ Consider which you think is best and why ■ Share conclusions and plan presentation

Drama Y9

Learning objective	Context	Process success criteria
To be able to accept, respond and reply creatively to Teacher In Role	Pollution	Remember to: ■ Use appropriately adapted language and movement ■ Use these to signify status and place ■ Don't show embarrassment ■ Sustain belief in your role ■ Develop the situation through your contributions ■ Move the drama on

Quality

The issue of quality is important when discussing success criteria. The purpose of students having success criteria is not to give them a simple fix-it list, but rather to remind them of those aspects of the task on which they most need to focus. Quality is ensured, not by the success criteria, but by the teacher's modelling and questioning, the level of discussion in the classroom and the quality of the different forms of feedback given (i.e. pairs, groups, teacher). In writing an effective characterisation, for example, it will be the examples given and the modelling of such writing, the quality of the process during the lesson, and the quality of the feedback offered to the student by peers or adults, that will finally ensure the overall quality of the student's work. Success criteria provide a basis for a dialogue to take place. Formative assessment begins once this dialogue is generated.

The Assessment for Learning section of the QCA website (www.qca.org.uk) stresses the importance of modelling quality through a variety of means, including:

- encouraging students to listen to the range of students' responses to questions;

- showing students the learning strategies;

- showing how the assessment criteria have been met in some examples of work from other students (not known to your students);

- encouraging students to review examples from anonymous students that do not meet the assessment criteria, in order to suggest the next steps to meeting the assessment criteria;

- using examples of work from other students in the class highlighting the ways in which it meets the assessment criteria or standards.

The Teaching and Learning in the Foundation Subjects (TLF) strand of the Key Stage 3 National Strategy devotes an entire module to the importance of modelling: *'Teachers use modelling to make skills, decisions and **processes** which are normally hidden, explicit to students. . . . This helps students to develop the confidence to use the **processes** independently'*

The impact of process success criteria

For the teacher

1   Planning process success criteria for individual lessons, *before writing the details of the activity*, has the following outcomes:

2   Planning time is often cut by approximately 50%, because success criteria essentially provide the lesson agenda. The activity details in the plan can, as a consequence, be abbreviated. Concerns about resourcing and modelling the focus points become more important than simply listing the tasks that will take place during the lesson. Overplanning the activity leads to a straitjacketing effect, where the success of a lesson can be mistakenly attributed to having got through all the planned tasks. The only thing that matters, and the main focus of the latest OFSTED framework, is whether learning is taking place in the lesson according to the objective.

3   The planned activity is more likely to match and therefore fulfil the learning objective.

4   Feedback to students is automatically focused around the success criteria, resulting in more specific and accurate targeting of needs.

For the students

1   Students have appropriate focus criteria while engaged in the task.

2   The criteria can be used as a focus for self-assessment, available for self-monitoring while engaged in the activity and afterwards (*Where am I achieving success? Where do I need to indicate that I need some help?*).

3   The success criteria form the feedback criteria for peer evaluation.

4   Success criteria help students develop a sense of what is and what is not important – vital for future independent learning.

The following accounts, from an English and a mathematics teacher, illustrate the particular way in which these teachers use process success criteria and the impact they have had on student learning. It is interesting to see the different approaches, as they correspond to the nature of the subject learning objectives: the mathematics teacher calls the success criteria 'instructions', because mathematics consists mainly of closed skills with corresponding chronological criteria. The English teacher has ingredient-style criteria but uses various formative assessment techniques (effective questioning, talking partners, no hands up, self- and peer assessment: all covered in later chapters of this book) to illustrate quality.

Mathematics teacher: Phillipa

'The introduction of process success criteria has had such a positive impact on my teaching and on my pupils' learning in a very short space of time. Higher GCSE Mathematics has been a focus for me as there are topics which require pupils to carry out lengthy calculations in order to solve problems correctly.

I tend to use the terms "instructions" or "method to . . ." in place of the phrase "process success criteria" to ensure my pupils understand what I am talking about. Together we decide what the instructions should be whilst I demonstrate by example. They enjoy choosing words that they understand as this gives them a sense of ownership of the topic and the lesson.

The most successful examples of the application of process success criteria have been with two higher-level topics: standard deviation and comparative pie charts. For both topics the pupils felt overwhelmed by the prospect of these lessons as they felt that it may be out of their reach academically but once we worked together to decide the "instructions", they felt that the work had become accessible to them.

Gradually, as they used the "instructions" again and again to answer questions, some of my pupils began to talk about their thoughts. They noticed the reasons why they were carrying out certain steps and using the "instructions" as a base for understanding as opposed to simply carrying out a method. I heard pupils saying:

"Oh, you square all the answers in step 2 because when you subtract the mean from each value, you get negative numbers . . . and you don't want to work with negative numbers, that's too hard." (Y10 pupil)

"I'm not quite sure but when you divide the area of the first pie chart by how many it stands for, you get how much space one person represents. That's right because in step 3, you times it by how many people the second pie chart stands for and that gives you its area." (Y10 pupil)

. . . and my favourite,

"Ooooooh, I get it!" (Y11 pupils)

Other pupils did not gain such an insight into the work but were confident in memorising the steps and answering questions without the process success criteria. Therefore all pupils leave the room with some feeling of achievement.

There has also been an increase in written workings in books and on practice examination questions. When I asked those who have been reluctant in the past to write their calculations why they are writing more, they explained that they were just doing what the instructions told them to do. As a result they have made themselves aware of where marks are allocated in examinations and have a clearer idea of what examiners are expecting of their written workings and how to gain full marks:

(continued)

"There are five steps here and the maximum mark you can get for this question is 5, so does that mean that each step is worth 1 mark?" (Y11 pupil)

This change in pupil learning, awareness and interaction has had a significant impact on my role in the classroom. My pupils know exactly what to do because it is in front of them and as a result there has been a decrease in pupil/teacher interaction and them asking me for help (more often they ask each other). I have more time to stand back and watch them learn. . . .'

Phillipa Rouet, Withywood Community School, Bristol

English teacher: Gina

Lesson One:
Year 7 (set 3). Learning focus: how language changes over time; how to work out definitions of unknown words. Context: *The Pied Piper* (narrative poetry)

'Pupils were first asked to list all the words that they did not know from the poem. Pupils were then given one minute thinking time to think about how they could work out meanings without the use of a dictionary.

In the past, without even realising it, I have only given pupils a few seconds of thinking time before answering it myself. Since extending the thinking time, in addition to the use of talking partners, I have found that pupils are a lot more responsive - they actually want to contribute their ideas, whereas they might have been less inclined to in previous lessons. Using the "no hands" strategy has also meant that pupils who had never contributed were able to comment and develop their ideas through my open questioning, thus building up their self-confidence. I am also able to get a more equal boy-girl ratio. I have found it very hard to judge the thinking time, however, as I have found that sometimes it is too long, leading to pupils becoming off-task.

Pupils' ideas were then fed back and written on the board.

I then gave pupils an exercise from *Fast Forward levels 5 to 6* (Sue Hackman). This activity gave them sentences with unknown words in bold *(e.g. 'Rival fans arrived, their **raucous** laughter and **intimidating** behaviour upsetting the local residents.)* From the context of the sentence, pupils had to try to work out the meanings before looking them up in the dictionary. Pupils had to fill in a table:

Word	What you think it means	Actual meaning
Matricide Sycophantic Raucous etc.		

(continued)

When pupils were unsure of the possible meaning, I gave them a context that they could understand/relate to better *(e.g. a Bristol City football match – How would the fans be behaving? What might they be doing?)*

Pupils were then asked to make comments regarding how they went about working out the meanings. These comments were added to the learning intention table (after I had asked pupils to tell me what the learning intention and context were):

Learning intention	Context	Success criteria: remember to. . .
Work out meanings of unknown words	The Pied Piper	■ Work out from the context ■ Look at the roots of words (etymology) ■ Look for patterns/combinations ■ Look for a prefix/suffix ■ Look for assonance/ onomatopoeia

'I had a colleague observing this lesson for ideas for Assessment for Learning. From her feedback, I found that she really liked the learning intention table. She said that through my process of what she called "let them have a go, consolidate ideas/success criteria, and execute", pupils picked up what to do quickly and, when asked to go through the same process with The Pied Piper, pupils understood the task and remained on-task. With this particular class, there are a few pupils that find it extremely hard to stay in their seats and who are rather disruptive in lessons. In this lesson, however, even these pupils were quiet and working hard. My colleague also said that my open questioning enabled pupils to develop their ideas and really think about the processes.'

Lesson Two:
Year 8 (set 2). Scheme of Work: Ballads

At the start of this unit, pupils were given the 'big picture' of this unit, which was displayed visually on the board as a spider diagram.

During the next few lessons, pupils read and analysed ballads for their conventions. This was done in the form of a table to allow pupils to compare the similarities and differences between ballads and their conventions:

	Ballad 1	Ballad 2	Ballad 3
Story			
Moral			
Chorus			
Rhythm			
Rhyme			
Shape			

(continued)

By repeating this exercise with three different ballads, pupils were able to remember and recognise common conventions of ballads.

'Pupils were unaware, whilst doing this, that they were gradually building up success criteria for the next activity.

At the start of this lesson, pupils were told that today they would be learning to write in the style of a ballad. At this, there were many complaints and groans from both boys and girls. They seemed rather apprehensive at such a seemingly mammoth task and I heard comments such as, 'Ah, Miss! Why do you always give us boring work?' and, 'I'm not doing that crap!' Such comments are rather disheartening, but I continued, asking pupils to give the lesson a chance.

Pupils were given the first and last verses of The Sad Story of Lefty and Ned to work on. Before planning and writing the ballad, pupils were asked, in pairs, to discuss the following questions:

1. What do the first and last verses tell us about the two characters?
2. There is a chorus in the ballad. What is it? Where does it occur?
3. What is the rhyming pattern in the ballad?
4. How would you describe the rhythm of the ballad?

As you can see, these questions relate to the particular aspects covered in the ballads grid. I then asked pupils to keep their hands down and I picked on the quieter members of the group, choosing equal numbers of boys and girls, to supply the answers.

After this discussion, pupils were asked for the learning intention, context and success criteria, which I wrote on the board as a table. I asked pupils to think about their answers to the above questions, in addition to the conventions of the previous ballads to form the success criteria. Pupils were able to supply these easily and confidently and were not afraid of me asking them to contribute, making them feel good about themselves and their knowledge. Pupils copied the table into their books as a reference to help them write their own version:

Learning intention	Context	Success criteria
To write a ballad	*The Sad Story of Lefty and Ned*	■ Rhyme scheme: AABB ■ Rhythm: fast – 4 beats per line ■ Chorus: last 2 lines of verse ■ 4 lines per verse ■ 7 new verses

Again in pairs, pupils were given a couple of minutes to discuss possible storylines, which were then shared with the class and written on the board as a reference.

Individually, pupils then had to plan their own story of Lefty and Ned in the form of a flowchart, which was then used, along with the success criteria, to write their ballad.

(continued)

After such a negative initial response to the idea of writing a ballad, pupils seemed to have forgotten their doubts and were eager to get started on their ballads. All were comfortable with the task set and with the success criteria that they had to adhere to. Much to their surprise, every pupil in the class actually enjoyed it and all were on-task. I know this because there are a few members of the class who are extremely apathetic towards their work and rarely complete or even start a piece of work. With this lesson, however, even these pupils succeeded in completing it. I was able to tell that pupils were on-task and enjoying it because they were discussing amongst themselves possible rhyming words and plot movement and all were happy to help each other. The lesson ended on a high for both myself and the pupils.

The effect of Assessment for Learning on my own teaching is that I am able to walk around the classroom more freely, ensuring that pupils are on-task and helping out when required. From this, I am able to see which pupils have understood the task and which pupils are still struggling with the idea. It also means that I don't have to keep repeating the same pieces of information over and over again because it has been written either on the board or in their books in a simplified, easy-to-understand format.

I am a newly qualified teacher: looking back to the Autumn term, I can now see that I was getting too bogged down with the learning objectives. I was making things too complicated and wordy for myself and for pupils. I was struggling with what the purpose of my lessons were, which must have made it really confusing for the pupils! I feel that this process has made me more focussed on the actual learning intention, which I am now able to quite easily separate from the context, an area which I struggled with at first. My learning intentions are much more specific now, giving my lessons a feeling of greater continuity. I also feel that I do not have to work quite so hard in lessons, because pupils are actually taking responsibility for their learning and I am able to enjoy the teaching process more and more.

Pupils are no longer confused as to the purpose of certain tasks or learning intentions and I feel that it has improved pupils' self-esteem because they are able to both contribute to class discussions (through the use of talking partners and thinking time) and are able to complete the work, as long as they follow the success criteria, to a high standard. I also believe that this heightened sense of self-efficacy has helped to improve my rapport with my classes because there is far less confrontation and a lot more opportunity for positive feedback and praise, which, of course, pupils love!! Overall, pupils are more actively involved in lessons having gained the ability to help their peers and become more involved in class discussions. Pupils have become more enthusiastic towards English as a result of the feeling of empowerment that they have gained.'

Gina L'Auria, Withywood Community School, Bristol

Sharing learning objectives with students: long- and short-term

Helping students make connections, see the big picture and establish what they already know

The sharing of learning objectives in lessons is now common practice. However, learning objectives are sometimes not broken down enough, so that students encounter the same long-term objective lesson after lesson. Even if specific learning objectives are given for each lesson, students often lose the 'big picture': how today's learning objective connects with what has been learnt so far and what is yet to come.

Many teachers instinctively tell students, verbally, what they will be learning at the beginning of a unit, but, unless students are given the coverage in writing, they are unlikely to remember the whole picture as the unit progresses, and the components then become discrete, unrelated elements. *Written* versions of the unit coverage are powerful tools to use at the beginning of a unit to establish what students already know and what they are interested in learning. Such lists also help students make important connections between concepts and skills and in their whole understanding of concepts and how to apply them to different situations, as well as keeping a mental track of what has been learnt and how it fits the big picture.

What to write

■ Mind-mapping is common practice at the beginning of a unit of work, giving students key words for which they write their current knowledge and understanding, making links where possible.

■ In 'picture dictation', used in New Zealand, students are each given a key word from the coverage on a card (e.g. the vocabulary for some work on liquids and solids) and asked to find out as much as they can about their word, through research or discussion. They create a 'physical' mind-map with the cards, standing up and holding their card (e.g. *'Who thinks their word is to do with liquids? Come and stand over here holding the cards up. . . Who thinks their word is to do with solids? Stand opposite the liquid people. . . . Who thinks their word connects the two? Stand between the two groups . . .'*, etc.) This is then transferred to a written class version. The class mind map is modified as the unit of work unfolds.

■ The coverage for the unit can simply be presented in the form of learning objectives, abbreviations, or learning objectives converted into questions, explained as the questions to be explored for this work.

■ For subjects such as history and geography, where much is already known from life experiences, it is highly motivating for students to be involved in the creation of the coverage. Giving students sub-headings and Post-it notes, on which they generate their own questions, usually results in much greater enthusiasm for the work to come. Students often bring in material from home, often from the Internet, and tend to pre-empt lessons with questions and comments. It seems obvious that more interest will be generated if one knows in advance where one is heading, but the traditions of the classroom have tended to result in coverage being gradually revealed.

Where to write it

■ If teachers stay in the same room, a flip chart can be used, with the different coverage for each class written on each page, so that each class has their coverage displayed throughout their lesson. This provides a useful visual tool throughout the lesson.

■ Where teachers are more mobile, use could be made of IT, such as a laptop and projector, to display coverage.

■ Some teachers prefer to issue students with a printed page showing the coverage, to attach to the inside front cover of their exercise book or folder. This can then be referred to at beginnings and ends of lessons. However, the big visual image in front of the class provides more opportunity for the teacher to point out connections, so both models together are useful.

Ongoing strategies

Establishing what students already know is vital, not only at the beginning of a unit of work, but also at the beginnings and throughout lessons. Rather than continually repeating the 'teach then apply' tradition, it is important to use open questions and talking partners (see chapter 3) to recall and reiterate current understanding. Alternatively, students can be asked to 'have a go' at an application before the specific teaching occurs. Subsequent teaching can build on needs clearly established from this initial exploration.

Sharing learning objectives and success criteria during lessons

Sharing learning objectives and success criteria leads to visible changes in the classroom: students and teachers are more focused on the learning than the activity, and students are more hardworking, cooperative, self-evaluative and confident. Success criteria form a framework for focus, self-evaluation, modelling and feedback.

Timing

To begin the lesson with the learning objective can kill it stone dead. It is often better to start by capturing the student's interest before revealing the learning objective.

Success criteria can be displayed in the following ways:

■ Just before the students start to work (if the activity takes place within the lesson), ask 'So what do you need to remember to focus on in order to achieve the learning objective?' Writing the success criteria in the words the students give back gives them ownership of the criteria.

■ Gathered one by one as the task requirements are taught, explored or modelled (a better approach if there are many steps involved and asking for recall of one of these would be unfair) 'So what do we have to do first? Next?'

■ Get the students to have a go at the task first, then ask them to tell you what they had to do first, next and so on (useful for mathematics calculations or any step-by-step procedure).

■ For application learning objectives which recur, pre-print the success criteria and Blu-tack them onto the whiteboard. Some teachers use a set of A3 laminated cards for this purpose. Alternatively, if the teacher stays in the same room, frequently used success criteria can be permanently displayed on the classroom wall.

Differentiation

Teachers often worry about differentiation and success criteria, imagining that there might be, say, four lists of success criteria because students are involved in different tasks. As long as teachers stick to the principle that all students should have access to the same learning objective, if they are roughly the same age, and the role of the teacher is to give them *access* to it, there will be generic success criteria for all students. For example, given the learning objective *'To write an account'*, it would be inappropriate to marginalise a group of students who cannot yet write more than a few sentences. The usual strategy here would be to give a supported version of an account, where some of it is already written.

Some teachers find it useful to highlight some of the success criteria, saying that these are the priorities. This strategy has had very good feedback from teachers reporting increased self-esteem and confidence in lower achievers, because these students still feel they are involved in the mainstream activity. Another strategy is to include, say, three possible outcomes within the success criteria at the last stage and tell students to either work through these or aim for one which will provide a challenge. For example:

Remember to:

- record the time taken each time
- compare results: either:

    describe rates of conduction; or

    apply conduction to less familiar situations; or

    give reasons for different rates of conduction using particles

Key principles

- There are two main types of learning objectives: *knowledge, concepts and skills* (taught specifics) and *applications* (the applying of the first within the 'whole context').
- Balancing the two types of learning objectives furthers learning.
- Learning objectives need to be explicitly separated from the context of the activity.

■ Students need to see, in written form, the aspects of a whole unit of study, in order to keep the connections between them.

■ *Process* success criteria are more powerful than *product* success criteria, although the final outcome should still be clear.

■ Success criteria need to be planned in advance.

■ Planning success criteria leads to more focused teaching and less overplanning of activities.

■ Success criteria should be, where possible, generic for all students, regardless of the task, as long as they all have access to the same learning objective.

■ Success criteria need to be articulated by students to give them ownership.

■ Quality comes from the teaching and feedback, not the success criteria.

■ We need to begin units of work and lessons by finding out what students already know (use talking partners rather than recall questions).

INSET ideas

1. Bring the last few weeks' short-term/Scheme of Work/lesson plans to a staff meeting and introduce the 'taught specifics' and 'application' learning objectives. Get teachers, in pairs or groups, to analyse their lessons and feed back on their findings. They could then together plan any adjustments to balance and feed back.

2. Using their short-term/Scheme of Work/lesson plans, teachers in pairs separate learning objectives from context (give them relevant pages from this chapter as a handout, for examples). Feed back findings and discuss.

3. Brainstorm current practice and ideas for giving students a way of seeing all the learning objectives to be covered for a particular area of study. Ask teachers to try out their own ideas or the suggestions on page 42. Feed back a few weeks later.

4. Introduce the findings about process success criteria and give examples. Get teachers to review their current practice through discussion. Go through the examples (see page 43) one at a time with the whole staff, giving them all the information except the success criteria. In pairs, they decide on the success criteria.

Decide together on the best success criteria, then compare to the success criteria given in the examples. If there is a discrepancy, discuss together why that might be. All this takes time, but it's worth it!

5. Next get teachers to bring along their short-term/Scheme of Work/lesson plans and, in pairs, take one lesson and decide learning objective, context and process success criteria. Pairs make fours, then all read them out. Discuss them as a whole staff, tweaking the words till they are acceptable (this might involve changing any part of the plan). Go round all groups. If this is a half-day session, get teachers to do another activity straight away, building on what they have learnt through these discussions. It should be quicker! Feed back findings again. Do it again with a third activity.

6. After this INSET, ask teachers to try planning one lesson in this way to begin with, and gradually apply to other lessons. Feed back in two weeks to discuss findings and ways forward.

7. Teachers share ways of finding out what students already know at beginnings of a unit of work or a lesson.

3 Questioning

Questioning is an area of formative assessment which, in many ways, encapsulates *'the active involvement of students in their own learning'*. Although improving teacher questions is a continual process, it is an area of formative assessment which can result in relatively rapid, positive changes in the classroom.

The Teaching and Learning in the Foundation Subjects (TLF) strand of the Key Stage 3 strategy is a useful resource for this important area of formative assessment.

This section includes three main elements:

(a) strategies for managing the classroom to enable effective questioning;

(b) ways in which questions can be framed to enable students to extend their thinking and learning;

(c) the role of the teacher in creating a supportive ethos.

(a) Management strategies

Wait time

Rowe (1974) found that teachers leave approximately one second before answering an unanswered question or asking someone else to answer it.

Increasing 'wait time' can be achieved by:

■ indicating the thinking time and asking for no hands up until the time is up;

■ asking for talking partner discussions for a given period of time before taking responses;

- asking students to jot their thoughts on paper for a given period of time before taking responses;

- simply leaving more time for processing to take place.

After a period of students getting used to a different expectation, extending wait time leads to the following:

- answers are longer;

- failure to respond decreases;

- responses are more confident;

- students challenge and/or improve the answers of other students;

- more alternative explanations are offered.

No hands up

Most teachers' lessons begin with a question-and-answer recall session of the whole class (e.g. '*So what were we talking about last week? Who can remember the elements involved in . . . ?*'). The typical response is that the same few students continually have their hands up and, in order to elicit the right answers, the teacher chooses the right students. If the wrong answer is given (usually students who would give the wrong answer don't have their hands up!) the teacher gives a side-stepping response and moves to someone who does.

Even if an open question is asked, hands shooting up while a student is in the process of thinking something through stops that process dead in its tracks. Many students have had this classroom experience so many times in their lives that, when a question is asked, they don't even begin the thinking process. Not only are they being interrupted in their thinking, but they are also having continual reinforcement that, compared to others, they are less able at this subject: the 'comparison effect' in action. When this happens, students gradually lose motivation and avoid investing effort in the subject, eventually opting out altogether.

Experimenting with 'no hands up' is a move towards a solution. *Anyone* can be asked to answer, which naturally raises the level of focus in the classroom. However, if the teacher continues to ask recall questions, more students are likely to be faced with the 'I don't know' prospect. Asking a better question is the aim here, but first a look at the power and impact of making 'talking partners' a constant feature of the classroom. . . .

Talking partners

Even if the question is a basic recall question *('In which layer of the leaf does photosynthesis take place?')*, a more effective approach than rapid fire is to ask the question, then ask students to talk to the person next to them for, say 30 seconds, to determine the answer. The answers are then gathered, with no hands up, from a number of pairs (with one student acting as spokesperson each time) until a full definition is compiled. When asking open questions *('What might be the reasons for this?')*, it is often useful to ask students to raise their hands if their partner had a good idea that they could tell the class.

Having 'talking partners' as a regular feature of lessons (especially beginnings) allows all students to think, to articulate and therefore to extend their learning. Shy, less confident students have a voice and the over-confident students have to learn to listen to others, so the benefits extend to a more respectful, cooperative ethos and culture: fundamental to the success of assessment for learning. We have tended to over-focus on individual students when they have responded to a question, so that the student's name is often repeated and maybe public congratulations given, thus reinforcing the comparison effect for those students who have not responded. With talking partners, the pair is asked to respond, which changes the emphasis from the student to the response.

Organising and training talking partners, regardless of their age, is essential. Some key points:

- Although the aim is for any student to successfully engage with any other student, this may not be possible if it is a new experience for them. Gender and friendship issues can get in the way, so pairs might need to be established for a set period of time, maybe changing each week, until the expectation is established.

- Simply asking students to talk to the person next to them can result in a number of students being without a partner. Even if the partners are set, it is important, at the beginning of a lesson, to quickly sweep around the room to make sure everyone knows who they will be talking to during those times ('you two, you two, you three . . .' etc). Absences mean that a number of students might be without a partner.

■ Some teachers model for students what it means to engage in a one-minute discussion (e.g. one person speaks and the other one listens, etc).

■ It can be useful to set class ground-rules for talking partners, group or class discussions. The following were used by one teacher:

Ground-rules for talking partners and discussion groups

■ Show you are listening by making eye contact.

■ Look at whoever is speaking.

■ Don't interrupt.

■ Don't shout.

■ Think about what the speaker is saying.

■ Hearing is waiting for gaps so you can speak . . . listening is when you can let go of what you want to say and listen to what is being said.

Snowballing and travelling

The Critical Skills Program uses Fig. 3.1 to describe the different kinds of learning styles and their related average retention rates. Teaching others is seen as the highest-order skill, the one where more deep learning occurs. Snowballing and travelling are strategies for enabling students to *explain* their thinking or teach others.

Snowballing: talking partners form fours and take turns explaining their ideas to each other.

Travelling: when students are involved in group discussion, one student from each group moves on to the next group after a given period of time. On arrival they have one minute to summarise the key points from their previous group, and the receiving group has one minute to explain their thinking to the newcomer. This rotation occurs at set intervals.

Fig. 3.1 Preferred learning styles

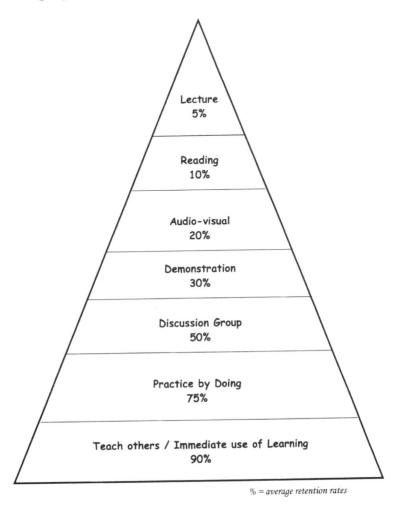

Lecture
5%

Reading
10%

Audio-visual
20%

Demonstration
30%

Discussion Group
50%

Practice by Doing
75%

Teach others / Immediate use of Learning
90%

% = average retention rates

Adapted from National Training Laboratories, Bethel, Maine. 1997

The six 'thinking hats'

Edward De Bono's 'thinking hats' approach is an effective way of getting students to answer questions from a variety of perspectives. Students are given a question and then given a particular hat with which to think about it. This makes the thinking more manageable and more directed. The approach is particularly useful when students are involved in answering more complex questions. A visual aid of the functions of the different hats is usually displayed in the classroom, or attached to the whiteboard for lessons (Fig. 3.2).

Fig. 3.2

Hat type	Examples
White hat thinking: involves facts, figures and information presented neutrally. This is about gathering information, so questions may include: *What information do we have? What is missing? What do we need? How do we get it?*	■ What has the land been used for previously? ■ How many people live there? ■ How will the water be transported?
Black hat thinking: involves caution, truth and judgement. This is about reality, identifying problems and avoiding mistakes. It promotes thinking about the validity of your line of reasoning, so questions may include: *Do the conclusions follow from the evidence? Is the claim justified? Will the plan work? What are the dangers of the plan?*	■ Will there be sufficient drainage? ■ Is a leisure centre really needed here?
Red hat thinking: involves emotions, feelings, hunches and intuition, and therefore allows people to put forward feelings without having to justify them, however mixed they are! Questions may include: *What do I feel about that decision? Is my gut reaction yes or no?*	■ Do I want a building in the middle of this area? ■ Do I think this design is too modern?
Yellow hat thinking: involves looking for the positives – the sunny day thinking – advantages, benefits or savings, but they must be justified! Questions may include: *What are the benefits? Why?*	■ What are the good things about having a leisure centre here?
Green hat thinking: involves creative thinking, exploration, proposals, suggestions and new ideas. It is about broadening the range of options before any one of them is pursued in detail, and does not require the logical justification of alternatives. Questions may include: *What would we ideally wish for? What alternatives are there?*	■ What else could we do with the space? ■ What about an adventure park? ■ Or some futuristic green houses?
Blue hat thinking: involves metacognition – thinking about thinking. It is about reflecting on the process rather than the decisions. Questions may include: *Where are we now? What is the next step? Is this the best way to decide?*	■ Was this a good way to go about making the decision? *(in Sullivan, 2003)*

(b) Framing the Question

❝ *More effort has to be spent in framing questions that are worth asking: that is, questions which explore issues that are critical to the development of students' understanding.* ❞

(Black et al., 2003)

Most importantly, these questions need to be **planned**. Teachers with highly effective questioning skills often reel off questions, it would appear, from the tops of their heads. The reality is nothing quite so instinctive. These teachers have simply planned their questions prior to the lesson. In Department meetings there needs to be agreement on:

- what questions we want to ask for a particular topic/unit;
- what are the most important questions;
- how each question will increase in challenge.

These key questions require space on lesson plans. They can be highlighted, underlined or made bold. They need to be easy to refer to.

In Fig. 3.3, *'before'* and *'after'* questions are listed by Dave Tuffin, a science teacher who had been involved in a long-term formative assessment research project. *'Before'* is how he used to frame questions. *'After'* is typical of the kind of question he would now ask, replacing recall questions with questions which are better designed for extending student learning and for students to demonstrate their understanding and knowledge (see page 63 for more of his ideas).

The approach is categorised each time to make it easier to apply the type of question to another topic or subject. The final column gives an example in another subject.

Original question	Reframed question	Strategy used	Example in another subject
How would you describe a good scientific prediction?	What do we need to consider before making a good scientific prediction?	*Asking for the elements to be involved in answering the question*	What do we need to consider before deciding how to characterise the mother in this novel?
Which word is used to describe energy types such as elastic, chemical and gravitational?	Why is the word 'potential' used to describe energy types such as elastic, chemical and gravitational energy?	*Providing the vocabulary and asking why it is appropriate or how it was arrived at*	Why does 3/11 + 8/11 = 1? Why is the word 'erosion' used to describe how coastal features are formed?
Which of these two questions did you consider to be the best?	Why did you consider question 3 to be a better question than question 1?	*Including an explanation*	Why is it easier to farm in lowland areas than upland areas?
How does the wave on the oscilloscope change when I turn this knob?	Can you use the words we have already come across to describe the changes to the wave on the oscilloscope screen?	*Providing vocabulary support*	Can you use the words duration, pitch and dynamics to explain how graphic notation works?
Which forms of exercise improve the efficiency of the heart?	Do you agree or disagree with this statement? *All forms of exercise improve the efficiency of the heart.* Give reasons for your answer.	*Setting a hypothesis to prove or disprove, with reasons*	Everything Henry VIII did improved the lives of ordinary people. Romeo and Juliet caused their own tragedies.
Why do you think there are so many people interested in reducing pollution in large cities such as London?	What argument would car drivers in London have against the wishes of the anti-pollution campaign who are trying to reduce the number of cars in the city?	*Asking a question to be answered from an opposing standpoint*	How would someone whose students were hungry determine morality?
What do plants need to grow?	Why is this plant healthy and this plant sick?	*Finding opposites and asking for explanation*	Why is this sentence better than this one? Why is this sum right and this one wrong?

(Tuffin, 2003)

Fig. 3.3 opposite

By reframing the question, the thinking will be increased considerably, but by asking for all students to think and articulate their thinking, given a short time to discuss their ideas with a partner, means maximum overall thinking and learning will take place.

Another versatile and commonly used strategy is to give a range of answers for students to discuss. They need to decide which are the right answers, which are close answers and why, and which answers can't be right but how they might have been arrived at, or which answers can't be right and why. This strategy has the potential for rich and fruitful follow up exploration. Some examples . . .

What is 5 squared?	Discuss these 'answers'. Give reasons for them: 3, 7, 10, 25, 125
Which physical activities improve the efficiency of the heart?	Weight-lifting, golf, darts, jogging, cycling, walking, swimming, skydiving, skiing
What did the Romans do for us?	Roads, trade, architecture, crops, sewers, laws, money, social harmony, learning

Bloom's Taxonomy

Bloom identified a hierarchy of questions that are extremely useful for helping teachers to move classroom questions beyond the literal and to support differentiation within the classroom. The following examples of Bloom's questions 'brought to life' are taken from the Brighton and Hove LEA publication *Questions Worth Asking* and the Manchester LEA publication *Questions*. The examples powerfully illustrate the differences between the different types of questions, enabling teachers to more easily apply them to their own classroom contexts.

Example 1: From 'Questions worth asking'

	What students need to do	Examples of possible question structures
Knowledge	Define, recall, describe, label, identify, match, name, state	*What is it called?* *Where does . . . come from?* *When did it happen? Who?* *What types of triangles are there?*
Comprehension	Translate, predict, explain, summarise, describe, compare (events and objects), classify	*Why does he . . . ?* *Explain what is happening in the crater. . . .* *So how is Tim feeling at this point?* *What are the key features . . . ?*
Application	Demonstrate how, solve, try it in a new context, use, interpret, relate, apply ideas	*What do you think will happen next? Why?* *So which tool would be best for this?* *Put the information into a graph.* *Can you use what you now know to solve this problem . . . ?*
Analysis	Analyse, explain, infer, break down, prioritise, reason logically, reason critically, draw conclusions	*What patterns can you see in the way these verbs change?* *Why did the Germans invade?* *What assumptions are being made . . . ?* *What is the function of . . . ?*
Synthesis	Design, create, compose, combine, reorganise, reflect, predict, speculate, hypothesise, summarise	*Compose a phrase of your own using a syncopated rhythm.* *What is the writer's main point?* *What ways could you test that theory?* *What conclusions can you draw?*
Evaluation	Assess, judge, compare/ contrast, evaluate	*Which slogan is likely to have the greatest impact?* *Should they develop the green-field or the brown-field site?* *Which was the better strategy to use?*

Example 2: From 'Questions'(Manchester LEA) – Year 6/7 Using *Boy* by Roald Dahl (1986)

Literal questions (recall and comprehension)	*What was the headmaster's name?* *Can you describe his appearance?* *Where were the students told to go after assembly?* *How old was Dahl at the time?* *How did Dahl feel when he first saw Mrs Pratchett?* *What kind of sweet jar did she find the dead mouse in?*
Application	*Can you compare Mrs Pratchett to a person who has frightened you?* *Write a paragraph about a frightening character either in a book you have read or that you have met. Describe their appearance, your feelings towards them and what they say or do that is frightening. Try to include some effective similes in your paragraph.*
Analytical	*How does the author make the headmaster appear frightening?* *Consider:* ■ *his appearance;* ■ *his relationship with the students;* ■ *the use of similes to describe him.* *How do you know that Dahl was frightened?* *Consider:* ■ *his feelings about Mr Coombes;* ■ *his feelings when he goes out to line up;* ■ *how the author describes the moments leading up to Mrs Pratchett identifying him;* ■ *how the author describes Thwaites' reactions.* *What do you think makes this a successful story? Use evidence from the text to justify your opinion.*
Synthesis	*Write the next part of the story.* *Rewrite the extract as an entry in Dahl's diary.*
Evaluation	*Would you like to go to this school? Give evidence from the passage for your answer.* *How do you think your headteacher would deal with a similar incident in your school?*

Problem-solving questions

Jos Elstgeest, in his chapter 'The right question at the right time' from the book *Taking the Plunge: how to teach science more effectively* (Harlen, 1985), makes some useful points about questioning in the context of science, which can be applied to many other subjects.

Elstgeest explains how we often ask students open questions too soon in the process of an investigation. For instance, asking them *'Can you make a plant grow sideways?'* is likely to elicit a 'yes' or 'no' response, or a plethora of random ideas about how to set up this experiment. We need to structure the order of questioning in science so that students are fully conversant with the characteristics and properties of the subject of experimentation. They are then in a position to be able to design experiments. If students have first found out as much as they can about what happens to plants in different circumstances, they will then be in a position to design a way to make one grow sideways.

Elstgeest (1992) suggests an order of questions as follows:

1   Start with **attention-focusing** questions (e.g. *What can you see? What is this? What do you know about it?*). This is the initial exploration stage.

2   Move on to **quantifying** questions (e.g. *How many? How long is it? How heavy is it?*). Students find out more about the objects using measuring skills.

3   Lead in to **comparison** questions (e.g. *Is it longer than . . . ? How much heavier is it than . . . ? In how many ways are your seeds alike and how do they differ?*). Observations are sharper as a result of these questions. Students are naturally classifying and ordering their observations and data.

4   Suggest **action** questions (e.g. *What happens if you place your cress seeds in damp sand? . . . if you place a cutting or twig in water? . . . if you hold your magnet near a match?*). Students are encouraged to experiment and investigate relationships between what they do and the reaction of the thing they handle. *'What happens if . . .'* questions should be preceded by an invitation to predict the outcome.

5   Students are now ready for **problem-posing** questions (e.g. *Can you find a way to make a plant grow sideways? . . . make a sinking object float? . . . separate salt from water?*). Students have become familiar with the possibilities, impossibilities and properties of the

objects under study. They are now capable of setting up for themselves hypotheses and situations to test them.

Encouraging students to generate their own questions

When students are involved in developing their own questioning skills, they are actively involved in their own learning. The findings from the Suffolk LEA (www.slamnet.org.uk) action research project indicated that students were:

- developing independence;
- taking more responsibility for their own learning;
- working through difficulties rather than asking for help;
- able to explain and express themselves more easily;
- thinking about what they were trying to achieve by asking questions;
- seeking explanations and alternatives more frequently;
- starting to manipulate their learning;
- reflecting on/evaluating their own understanding and often taking it further.

Effective teaching and questioning includes effective modelling as a constant feature of lessons. Without modelling, students often have no idea of what is expected of them and do not further their understanding by seeing models of excellence. Effective modelling involves:

- 'thinking aloud' and being totally explicit about the thinking process;
- showing precisely *how*;
- making visible and explicit the 'structure' of the process, concept or knowledge;
- breaking down the process into a series of manageable steps;
- encouraging students to think for themselves or to ask their own questions;
- encouraging students to contribute;
- after modelling, scaffolding the learning through shared or guided activities;

■ building-in time for students to reflect on the process;

■ enabling students to do it independently.

(Key Stage 3 National Strategy, 2003)

The following description of a teacher asking students to develop their own questions illustrates a number of other strategies in action: sharing success criteria, talking partners, teacher prompting and modelling: students involved in the assessment process. The lessons show how formative assessment informs planning: the students' understanding is clearly revealed, giving pointers for future lessons.

An excerpt from *Assessment for Learning* (Black et al., 2003):

The students were eventually going to engage in a piece of autobiographical writing. The lesson entails giving a Year 7 mixed-ability class a brief passage called "The Sick Boy", which the teacher had adapted from Laurie Lee's novel Cider with Rosie, *so that it was devoid of detail of any kind, giving the barest outline of events with little attention to the vocabulary or, to use the technical term, lexical density. The students were asked to annotate the text with any questions they would like to put to the author to make the text more interesting. The ideas were shared with partners as the teacher went around the class listening to the questions and prompting students to think of further ideas.*

*The questions were then collected and discussed by the class as a whole. The class were then read the actual extract form Laurie Lee's book and the students were asked to see how many of the questions were answered in the original text. This too was discussed. The lesson ended and was followed by another lesson immediately after lunch in which the questions were categorised as **factual**, such as 'What was someone's name?', or as **reactional empathetic**, such as 'How did this make the mother feel?' Lee's passage answered both types of question. These types of question were then used as the basis for the criteria by which the students' work was to be assessed. In other words, the teacher made explicit, as they began to write, that the features they had identified as helping to make the piece of writing more interesting would be the features by which their own work would be judged.*

In the next account, a teacher describes his experiences of improving students' questioning skills and then summarises his overall findings about seeking to improve all aspects of questioning in his classes.

Science teacher: Dave

'To improve the quality of student's questioning in the classroom I introduced the following strategies:

- Students generate their own questions for each other and a parallel class. These questions were written by students in small groups, using one of two approaches:
  - (a) Students are given small areas of the topic under discussion and are asked to write five questions on that topic. Each group nominates a spokesperson who reads out their group's questions, and the class discuss the merits of each question; the best two (majority decision) are chosen. This provides us with at least ten good questions for the remainder of the lesson or for homework.
  - (b) Students are asked to develop three questions on a wider topic, such as a unit on energy. After a class discussion, the best questions are written on the board and given for homework or to another class. The authors of the questions are expected to provide answers to their questions.
- Students analyse a series of questions on a related topic and discuss the merits of each question. A significant element here is that students are asked to write their thoughts about some homework questions they have been given. Typical question from me are: *'Did this question make you think more about work we have covered in class?'*, *'Do you think this question was an effective way of testing your understanding of this topic?'*
- Students modify questions on worksheets and from textbooks in order to improve their learning. They were told to modify questions based on what they already know and to match their own syllabus.

Students loved the idea of changing questions generated by teachers and textbook authors and were sure that their answers were 'better'. The focus group took to this particularly well. After several attempts at modification of questions, they realised that their answers were probably just more appropriate for their needs than those they were changing.

Students really enjoyed developing their own questions. The standard of the questions was poor to start with, but soon developed. They clearly recognised which questions were simply asking for recall of facts and those which required more lateral thinking or application of factual information.

When analysing what makes a good question, the students were generally in agreement, despite one or two choosing questions which meant less homework! The students did not always choose the most appropriate or thought-provoking questions. This is happening slowly.

Questioning is one of the most basic techniques for testing understanding and improving learning. I certainly did not spend enough time developing questions prior to commencing my formative assessment training. Now, I jot down ideas for questions when preparing the week's lessons, giving myself time to think about them and modify them as appropriate. Alternatively, I use the quiet time before school begins to write questions on the board for

(continued)

each class. As the day goes on, I have the questions in full view and modify them. The questions are also modified during the lesson on occasions and my sixth form tutor group is beginning to help alter my questions to make them more challenging. Not until you analyse your own questioning do you realise how poor it can be. I found myself using questions to fill time and asking questions which required little thought from the students. When talking to students, particularly those who are experiencing difficulties, it is important to ask questions which get them thinking about the topic and will allow them to make the next step in the learning process. Simply directing them to the 'correct answer' is not useful.'

(Dave Tuffin, 2003)

(c) Creating a supportive climate

When students get an answer wrong, or it is not the answer the teacher wanted to hear, it is important to avoid 'put downs', either by tone of voice or words used. When challenging questions are asked, it is useful to make students aware of what you are expecting: *'I expect this to be a question many of you will have to really think about. I'm not expecting right answers, just your thoughts at this moment. Say anything and we'll see what we can pool together.'*

Some effective ways of responding to wrong and right answers to encourage more thinking and less reliance on the teacher include:

- **Gathering**: *'Thank you. Does anyone have a different idea/answer/agree/ disagree/have something to add?'* until a collective agreement is reached

- **Asking for explanation of wrong answers so that incorrect answers are used to advantage** e.g.:

    Teacher: *Is this apple dead or alive?*

    Student 1: *Dead.*

    Teacher: *Why do you think it's dead?*

    Student 1: *When it was on the tree it was part of the living tree, but it's not now.*

    Teacher: *Who agrees? Is there anyone who disagrees?*

    Student 2: *We don't know that it's dead . . . a bit could still be alive.*

Student 3: *I think that's possible, because if you put the pips in the ground they'd grow . . .*
(from *How do they walk on hot sand?* Suffolk LEA, 2002)

- **Echo**: *'Seventeen.' 'Who would like to agree? Who would like to disagree?'*

- **Stalling**: *'Hold that thought. Let's carry on and then come back to that later'* , giving a chance for the student to self correct after more discussion has illuminated things.

- **No pressure**: *'So what might the answer have been? Say anything you like.'*

The TLF strand of the National Strategy offers an interesting and highly useful section on **Alternatives to Questions** within its module on Questioning (Handout 4.2) to extend the possibilities given so far (Fig. 3.4).

Fig 3.4

Alternative Strategy	Example
Invite students to elaborate	*'Would you say a little bit more about that.'* *'I am not sure I know what you mean by that.'*
Speculate about the subject under discussion	*'I wonder what might happen if . . .'*
Make a suggestion	*'You could try . . .'*
Reflect on the topic	*'Perhaps we now have a way of tackling this next time you . . .'* *'Let's bring this altogether . . .'*
Offer extra information	*'It might be useful to know also that . . .'* *'I think that I have read that . . . .'*
Reinforce useful suggestions	*'I especially liked . . . because . . .'*
Clarify ideas	*'We can tell this is the case by . . .'*
Correct me if I'm wrong	*'But I thought we had agreed that . . .'* *'So now perhaps we all believe . . .'*
Echo comments / Summarise	*'So you think . . .'* *'Jane seems to be saying . . .'*
Non-verbal interventions	Eye contact, a nod, or raised eyebrows to encourage extended responses, to challenge or even to express surprise.

We need to aim for a supportive ethos where even wrong answers are seen as useful (if they are followed by discussion and exploration) and students can say 'pass' to a question without fear of failure. However, our classroom traditions have for many years encouraged students to feel demoralised about their abilities, so the supportive climate needs to be carefully developed.

Key principles

- Students need approximately five seconds' wait time.
- 'No hands up' increases wait time and student focus.
- Having talking partners/groups before responding to questions enables all students to participate, think and articulate.
- Using a range of different types of questions leads to enhanced student understanding
- Encouraging students to develop their own question furthers their independence as learners.
- Effective questioning involves effective modelling.
- Teachers need to create a supportive climate so that 'put downs' are avoided and students can articulate their ideas without fear of failure.

INSET ideas

1. Present the whole chapter to staff and discuss perceived strengths and needs in existing practice. Focus particularly on recall questions and their impact.
2. Focus on talking partners for one week and feed back findings. Pick up issues developed in the chapter.
3. Plan together some good questions for one lesson each, based on one or more of the ideas given on pages 56–7. Work on these planned questions together before using them in the lessons. Use them with one or two minutes' talking partners each time and report back findings.
4. Decide either individually or together which area most interests you and set a period of time to experiment (not too short to allow for difficulties/students getting used to it, etc). Feed back findings, analysing impact on learning and teaching. Share specific ways of asking questions which have been successful.
5. Continue trialling, building up different elements and techniques from the chapter.

4 What matters about feedback

> 6 The most powerful single moderator that enhances achievement is feedback. 9

(Hattie, 1992)

Whether feedback is oral or written, there are some key features which can be drawn from a great deal of classroom research.

The impact of traditional feedback on student motivation and achievement

When the Black and Wiliam (1998) review of formative assessment was published, the aspect which received most media attention was their findings about teachers' feedback to students. The traditional forms of feedback have, in many cases, led to regression in students' progress. Key negative elements are the giving of grades for every piece of work and external rewards, such as merit marks (see Chapter 1). Also loaded with potential to reinforce for students a sense of failure and lack of ability are: the teacher's tone of voice; body language; how difficulty with learning is talked about; the over-use of teaching assistants with certain students; and the words used by teachers when interacting with students.

Hargreaves, McCallum and Gipps (2001), in their research of feedback strategies used by teachers, found a range of 'approval' and 'disapproval' strategies. Non-verbal strategies for expressing *approval* included the teacher nodding, making eye contact, smiling, laughing, putting an arm around or patting the student and taking on a mild manner in order to be approachable. Non-verbal means of expressing *disapproval* included pulling faces, staring hard, clicking fingers or making disapproving noises. All of these strategies give clear messages to students about how the teacher feels about their ability.

The LEARN Project (University of Bristol, 2000 – see www.qca.org.uk) consisted of interviews with over 200 students between Years 3 and 13 about their perceptions of assessment. The key findings were:

- Students were often confused by effort and attainment grades.
- Students sometimes felt that their effort was not recognised by teachers.
- Students preferred feedback that was prompt and delivered orally.
- Students were often unable to use feedback effectively.
- Students felt that feedback that was constructively critical helped improve their performance.

My own findings have been:

- Students believe that the purpose of marking is for the teacher to find out what they have got right or wrong, rather than for their own benefit.
- Students are rarely given time to read marking comments.
- Students often cannot read or understand the teachers' handwriting or comments.
- Students are rarely given time to make any improvement on their work because of the teacher's feeling of pressure to get on with coverage.
- Many teachers worry that giving pupils 'time' to make any improvements on their work at the start of the lesson means a 'bitty' and informal or chaotic start.

A closer look at grading

‘ *Teachers should be aware of the impact that comments, marks and grades can have on learners' confidence and enthusiasm and should be as constructive as possible in the feedback that they give.* ’

(Assessment Reform Group, 2002)

Ruth Butler (1988) carried out a controlled experimental study in which she set up three ways of giving feedback to three different groups of same age/ability students:

- marks or grades
- comments
- marks or grades and comments (the most common approach by UK teachers)

The study showed that learning gains (measured by exam results) were greater for the comment-only group, with the other two groups showing no gains. Where even positive comments accompanied grades, interviews with students revealed that they believed the teacher was 'being kind' and that the grade was the real indicator of the quality of their work.

Giving grades or marks for every piece of work leads to inevitable complacency or demoralisation. Those students who continually receive grades of, say, B or above become complacent. Those who continually receive grades of B- or below become demoralised. Interestingly, girls and boys find different reasons for any apparent failure. Dweck (1986) found that girls attributed failure to lack of ability. This was because teachers' feedback to boys and girls was such that it would lead to girls feeling less able, while enabling boys to explain their failure through lack of effort or poor behaviour.

In marking students' work with grades (competitive task orientation), teachers can be said to have focused students continually on the level of their ability compared to their peers. With a focus on feedback against the learning objectives of the *task*, however, students are enabled to improve realistically against past performance. It is important, of course, to know how one's performance compares with one's peers or against set criteria, but when this is the feedback for *every* piece of work, complacency or demoralisation sets in, thus impeding progress.

Many studies have shown that work marked by 'comment-only', with grades given only at end of units, increases motivation and achievement – findings which cannot be ignored.

On the whole, feedback has been a mainly negative experience for most students. Token comments at the bottom of work praising effort do not fool students, because the grades or rewards, and spelling and grammar corrections, tell students the 'truth' about their work.

What we now know about effective feedback

1. Focus feedback on the learning objective/success criteria of the task

Teachers have, in the past, apparently focused their written feedback on four main elements: presentation, quantity, surface features of any writing (especially spelling) and effort. Most school assessment policies also draw significant attention to these four main elements, which reinforces this practice. While these aspects are important, we have *over*emphasised them, so that the main focus of the lesson has been marginalised. What you put in is what you get out, so the message to students has been clear: get these things right and you will do better.

Effective feedback involves being explicit about the marking criteria. The other four features should be attended to every now and again rather than at every stage, and this needs to be reflected in any whole-school assessment policy.

2. Aim to close the gap

Sadler (1989) established three conditions for effective feedback to take place:

> *The learner has to (a) possess a concept of the standard (or goal, or reference level) being aimed for, (b) compare the actual (or current) level of performance with the standard, and (c) engage in appropriate action which leads to some closure of the gap.*

Improvement suggestions, therefore, need to be focused on how best to close the gap between current performance and desired performance, specific to the learning objectives in hand.

3. Give specific improvement suggestions

Kluger and DeNisis's (1996) research review showed that feedback only leads to learning gains *when it includes guidance about how to improve*. Terry Crooks (2001), as a result of his review of literature about feedback and the link with student motivation, concluded that:

the greatest motivational benefits will come from focusing feedback on:

- *the qualities of the student's work, and not on comparison with other students;*

- *specific ways in which the student's work could be improved;*

- *improvements that the student has made compared to his or her earlier work.*

Specific and *improved* are two key words in Crook's recommendations. We have tended to be too general in the past to be helpful to students (e.g. *'some good words here'* or broad targets such as *'remember to include more detail in your prediction*). We have also tended to focus feedback on *correction* rather than *improvement*.

It is often the case that, instead of giving specific, concrete strategies to help students move from what they have achieved to what we want them to achieve, teachers instead simply reiterate the desired goal – a reminder prompt. For example, *'You need to improve these two long sentences,'* merely reiterates the learning goal of *'To be able to write effective long sentences'*. Better advice would be, for instance, *'Improve these two long sentences, using some short noun phrases, such as* old features, thin lips blue, grating voice *or similar.'* Giving 'for instances' and specific advice is key to the quality of an improvement suggestion.

4. Students make the improvement suggested

The traditional model of feedback is to make suggestions for improvement which one hopes will be taken account of when the same learning objective is revisited at a later date. The main reason that comments appear over and over again on students' work is because students have not had an opportunity either to (*a*) carry out the improvement on that piece of work, according to the specificities of the improvement suggestion, or (*b*) revisit the skill in another context quickly enough. Only when this takes place will the improvement become embedded and able to be applied in further contexts. As Black and Wiliam (1998) found: *'For assessment to be formative, the feedback information has to be **used**.'*

5. Relinquishing control

In most classrooms, the *teacher* defines the goal, judges the achievement and tries to close the gap between achieved and desired performance. Formative assessment research emphasises the importance of the involvement of the *student*, so we need to be careful not to oversimplify the process of giving effective feedback, leaving the student with no stake in the process. We need to model effective marking, aiming to gradually relinquish control so that students are trained to be effective self- and peer markers and assessors.

Teachers' findings

The teachers in the Black et al. study stopped giving grades and focused on giving students improvement suggestions which were specific to the learning objective of the work (e.g. *'Well explained so far but add reasons why the Haber process uses these conditions'*) rather than general (e.g. *'Well explained but you could have given more detail'*). One teacher said:

'At no time during the first 15 months of comment-only marking did any of the students ask me why they no longer received grades. It was as if they were not bothered by this omission. I found this amazing, particularly considering just how much emphasis students place on the grades and how little heed is taken of the comments generally. . . . When asked by our visitor how she knew how well she was doing in science, one student clearly stated that the comments in her exercise book and those given verbally provide her with the information she needs. She was not prompted to say this!!'

(Black et al., 2003)

In summary

The Assessment Reform Group (2002), in *Assessment for Learning: Ten Principles*, said, as a result of collating the research about feedback:

‘ *Assessment that encourages learning fosters motivation by emphasising progress and achievement rather than failure. Comparison with others who have been more successful is unlikely to motivate learners. It can also lead to their withdrawing from the learning process in areas where they have been made to feel they are "no good". Motivation can be preserved and enhanced by assessment methods which protect the learner's autonomy, provide some choice and constructive feedback, and create opportunity for self-direction.* ’

Key principles

- Feedback needs to be focused on the learning objective of the task and not on comparisons with other students.

- Verbal and non-verbal language from the teacher give powerful messages to the student about his or her ability.

- Grading every piece of work leads to demoralisation for lower achievers and complacency for higher achievers.

- We need to give *specific* feedback focusing on success and improvement, rather than correction.

- We need to focus improvement suggestions on closing the gap between current and desired performance.

- Students need opportunities to make improvements on their work.

- We need to train students to effectively self- and peer assess their work.

INSET ideas

1. Get paired teachers to observe each other teaching any lesson for thirty minutes, taking notes under the following headings: *Body language/verbal language/tone of voice which boosts or lowers self-esteem.* Pairs compare notes after both have been observed and present findings at a staff meeting. Implications of the findings need to lead to action.
2. Ask students to write their opinions about grading and written feedback and compare findings at a meeting.
3. As a staff, trial comment-only marking (grading only at the end of units) if grades are normally given for every piece of work.

5 Quality feedback: practical implications

' Learners need information and guidance in order to plan next steps in their learning. Teachers should: pinpoint the learner's strengths and advise on how to develop them; be clear and constructive about any weaknesses and how they might be addressed; provide opportunities for learners to improve upon their work. '

(Assessment Reform Group, 2003)

Creating a school feedback policy

Before exploring the different types of feedback in depth, it seems appropriate to look at all elements of feedback as a whole, to establish a coherent school framework and policy. Many schools have a 'marking' policy. By renaming it a 'feedback' policy, oral feedback and student involvement can be legitimately included and valued. Marking is an especially difficult area, and many of the traditions of marking have caused *regression* in student achievement. Some of the problems are:

■ Teachers feel that they should be marking students' work as a measure of their worth: for accountability purposes, rather than to give feedback.
The purpose of marking should of course be to give feedback to students about their work.

■ Teachers feel that the quality of their feedback is measured by how much they have written on the student's work.
Research shows that too much information about too many aspects is inaccessible and demoralising.

■ Teachers feel that oral feedback is vital, but somehow not as valid as written marking and is difficult to do in a class of 35 or where groups need constant teacher attention.

Oral feedback is always more powerful, because it is tailor-made to the individual needs of the learner, but is usually unmanageable

■ Teachers feel guilty if every piece of work is not marked thoroughly.
A whole-school rationale in an agreed policy enables teachers to feel confident about their feedback

■ Teachers wonder whether their marking really makes any impact on students' progress: a soul-destroying experience.
Students need to be involved in the assessment process and to make improvements on the actual work on which the improvement suggestion was written.

We need, therefore, to establish an agreed policy for feedback throughout the school, following the same principles but modifying them for each department. A summary of key principles is the common starting-point. For instance:

Comment-only feedback

Principles

When giving feedback, either orally for a practical subject in the course of the lesson, or when marking student's work, it seems that several conditions need to apply to establish an effective model of feedback from teacher to student and students together:

■ Students need to know the learning objectives of the task and then how far they have fulfilled them.

■ Students then need to know, in relation to the learning objective, what they could have achieved, or where to go next.

■ Advice about spelling, handwriting and so on should not be mentioned for every piece of work, or students will be overloaded with information and focused on the same few criteria every time.

■ They then need to be shown how to 'close the gap' between current and desired performance. 'Shown' in this context would ideally include an invitation to include the student's perceptions and strategies.

■ Finally, and most importantly, students need *time* to make the suggested improvement.

A set of similar principles would be necessary for defining practice for giving grades or any other summative information. One school's concerns were addressed in the following way for two of the issues:

Concern that parents would think that books were not being marked frequently:
Led to . . . a letter home to parents explaining the new marking policy.

Concerns about how staff would be able to write reports or complete school tracking data with fewer marks in their markbooks:
Led to . . . (a) put grades in mark books but don't always share with pupils;
(b) only make a note of those who 'achieved significantly above or significantly below';
(c) use markbooks in a different way – to write comments rather than just grades.

Some possible sub-headings for the 'Strategies' section of the policy are suggested below, each of which needs to be agreed across departments, or modified by individual departments according to the same key principles:

1. Grading

2. Oral feedback

3. Marking techniques:
   (a) acknowledgement marking
   (b) sampling
   (c) marking together
   (d) comment-only marking

4. Self- and paired marking (see Chapter 6)

Unravelling the elements

1. Grading

It is becoming more and more common to grade every piece and enter these in a mark book, but only to write or share a final grade with the student *at the end of the unit.* The previous chapter explains the research about grading.

For departmental consistency, students should be clear about the criteria for the giving of grades. It is useful for each department to develop a folder of work which exemplifies good marking and which also contains sample pieces of work at particular levels or grades. Departments can also agree common units of work – for example, termly – which will be marked in detail to departmentally agreed criteria. These can form the focus of termly student review sessions.

Although grades should not be given for every piece of work, students should be aware of the wider context of the level or grade they should be working towards and the specific criteria which they need to be focusing on in order to reach that goal. How students reach these goals needs to be a combination of teacher modelling, ongoing dialogue with teachers in lessons, and self- and peer assessment.

2. Ongoing oral feedback

With practical subjects, and during the course of any lesson, teachers demonstrate quality through their modelling, but it is important to use the principles of formative assessment in any dialogue with students. The *'success and improvement'* approach outlined in the previous chapter and later in this chapter is instinctive for many teachers. However, making sure that both the acknowledgement of where success has been achieved and the improvement suggestions focus on **the learning objective** of the task is not always instinctive. We often overload students with too many criteria to improve aspects they might not have been asked to focus on. Limiting the criteria means that skills can be further developed. Modelling success and improvement against learning objectives acts as training for students to be able to use this approach in their own marking and paired marking.

The following example of quality oral feedback is given in *Good Assessment in Secondary Schools* (OFSTED, 2003):

Over the 60 minutes of an art lesson, the teacher gave detailed attention to each student. Occasionally, where the student declared the work to be finished, she pinned the painting on the wall and they looked at it together – in one case from the other side of the room – checking to see whether it had indeed reached a conclusive point or if more could be done. 'Have you got the foreground right?' 'Those colours look a bit strong – is that what you want?'(Checking against the success criteria.) 'Perhaps you could have another look at your source material.' (Giving an improvement suggestion.) Through such exchanges it was easy to see how the department has created an ambience similar to that of art school: from the beginning of Year 7, students are encouraged to talk seriously about their work and this quickly affects positively their attitude to the subject.

Difficulties

Oral feedback is of course the most powerful form of feedback any student can receive, but only practical subjects offer teachers and students *continual* opportunities for one-to-one oral dialogue during lessons. Oral feedback from peers, as a one-to-one experience, therefore, is a vital element in the feedback dynamic.

Oral feedback still takes place in other subjects, but usually from teacher to students in a whole-class setting, occasionally with groups during a lesson, and often at the end of a lesson or the beginning of the next. At this time teachers tend to go through completed work, talking about processes and answers, discussing and reviewing any misconceptions and modelling successes for the class as a whole.

Some solutions

(*a*) Structure for an end-of-unit lesson

A successful strategy used by teachers to allow classroom time for ongoing individual dialogue between teachers and students is to plan a lesson for the end of a particular long- or short-term unit of work, in which oral feedback can be given to individuals by both peers and the teacher.

The following example of this approach is a summary of a section from the excellent Birmingham Key Stage 3 *Assessment for Learning* video, involving Golden Hillock School with teacher Pete Weir:

Context: Text analysis – Y8

The learning objectives covered for this work are written on the whiteboard. These are the different elements of text analysis. The students have completed essays to use as the focus for the lesson. These have already been peer-assessed.

1. The students are given a grid sheet with two headings, as follows:

    Successes   **Evidence**

2. The teacher explains that the learning objectives worked on are on the board and that students should decide which elements they believe they have succeeded in and where, in their essay, they have demonstrated this, e.g. PQE (Point, quote, explain) in the success column, with an example from the essay to illustrate this in the evidence column.

(continued)

3. As the students complete the sheet, the teacher engages briefly with individuals, helping them to decide what to choose, clarifying, etc.

4. The students are then asked to decide which areas to target for improvements on their essays and for future improvements.

Although the clip ends at this point, students could then be asked to make the specific improvement for homework and keep a record of their targets for this work which can be focused on in future lessons.

(Birmingham Advisory and Support Service, 2003)

(b) Discussing course criteria: success and short-term targets

Ongoing dialogue with GCSE students can be difficult to manage, as there is so much coursework to be discussed. Making time while the coursework is in process is important. Again, making sure the student has the specific course criteria, in a written form, so that they can track their own progress and make judgements about successes and improvement needs means the time devoted to discussion can be better streamlined: the students take the lead in the ongoing dialogue in lessons. Within the context of the wider aim, having short-term targets feeds motivation.

(c) Regular review sessions between teacher and student

Many schools have introduced individual review session with individual students, say once a term, where teachers talk with students about what they have achieved and what they still need to target in order to reach the next level. It is clearly more effective if the student first makes a judgement about these things on an appropriate form, so that the meeting has the teacher as the 'mentor'. By far the most powerful set-up is when subject teachers meet with their pupils in this way, although it is often the case that the form tutor engages with the student. Clearly, the global approach leads to general and less effective targeting. Review weeks are a possible solution, where all lessons in a week consist of teacher/student group conferencing.

Another, more practical possibility is that subject teachers and students identify one key piece of work (an application) to be taken to the review, on which both teacher and student record their opinion of achievement and targets needed (students could write this in lesson time). The form tutor can then more confidently work through the pieces of work, discussing targets with the student. However, what is missing with this approach is the form teacher's ability to talk about how specific targets might be met for each subject.

Marking techniques

(a) Acknowledgement marking

The tick or initial is appropriate:

- when enough oral feedback took place during the course of the lesson for the basic needs of the learning objective to have been met;

- when the work was self- or pair marked;

- when the work is not designated for comment-only quality marking (see OFSTED quote below).

(b) Sampling

Finding time to mark student work is a major headache for secondary teachers. Choosing to mark a certain number of pieces in depth seems to be the way forward, with the remaining work self- or peer marked or acknowledgement marked:

‘ *This . . . raises the question of manageability, especially for teachers who take a large number of groups, as is the case for many teachers of music and religious education, for instance. The problem of manageability is being tackled successfully in some schools through systems for staggering marking or for sampling – for example, by marking only three classes' work each week, or that of 5–6 students in each group in one week, or marking in depth selected items only.* ’

(OFSTED, 2003)

One system of sampling involves creating mixed-ability marking groups. The teacher marks, by using the success and improvement approach, only one group's work per lesson, keeping track of the groups with a simple grid, colour coding or similar. Because a range of ability is dealt with each time, the teacher has a balanced representation of the class's understanding, misconceptions and future needs. Feedback subsequently given to the class build on the teacher's perceptions of needs.

(c) Marking together

When work can be profitably marked together in a whole-class setting (e.g. closed exercises) this cuts out a layer of often unnecessary marking, where wrong answers simply demoralise students. By going through the answers and related processes, students mark their own work, self-correcting where necessary, and enhancing the learning possibilities.

(d) Comment-only feedback: oral and written

The *success and improvement* strategy is recommended for comment-only marking, with time allocated for students to make selected improvements. There are two paths to follow with improvement suggestions written on work:

Making improvements to the marked work: these relate to the specifics of the piece and students are expected to make the suggested improvement on that piece either for homework or at the beginning of the next lesson (particularly effective for maximising achievement of developing specific skills and concepts).

Targets over a period of time: these relate to improvements which could be made against the learning objectives of the piece in any context.

Comment-only marking: the detail

(a) Making improvements to the marked work

The success and improvement strategy for comment-only marking (looking for, say, three successes and one improvement point against the learning objective) has been widely trialled in many schools, throughout the UK, with a great deal of success, often leading to higher test levels within a year, but, most importantly, equipping students with the ability to become more independent judges of their own successes and improvement needs.

What kind of learning objective works best?

The strategy is best used with specific lesson objectives rather than applications. Applications have many criteria, because they bring together all the skills learnt, so looking for limited success and improvement points can be difficult.

Identifying success with closed skills (e.g. following the steps in a specific mathematics procedure or algorithm) is simply a matter of matching the steps or answers against the success criteria, so identifying a limited number of successes would be a nonsense. Where the skill is open, however (e.g. using a range of effective similes/creating a fair test), it is useful to look for the best examples of achievement, and also one which could be improved. Identifying the most effective or successful examples enables excellence and quality for that student to be modelled and celebrated.

The strategy has a suggested starting point of three successes and one improvement per student. This orthodoxy is a necessary training stage. Eventually, of course, we want students to be able to identify any number of successes or improvement needs in their work, but, in the initial stages, for most day-to-day work, focusing on only a few elements allows greater development of the skill or concept in question.

Suggested 'success and improvement' steps

The following steps are suggested first stages, in which the teacher holds the control while modelling the process. The next chapter deals with students taking over much of the process, looking for their own successes and making improvements where they can.

1. Whole-class marking

The teacher takes several pieces of work from another class, photocopies them onto acetate and uses these for whole-class lessons in which three successes and an improvement suggestion are made by the class and the teacher together. The discussion over which places are best and how to help the student improve provides an excellent opportunity for quality analysis.

2. Mark individual work (only one or two classes a week to begin with)

Finding successes
Once the students are used to the strategy, the teacher marks individual work in this way: s/he finds the three **best** places in the student's work which link with the learning objective and highlights, circles or underlines these. This avoids having to write things which might be inaccessible to the student and enables the student to identify success immediately. All students should receive the same number in order to avoid the comparison effect. These successes should be within the context of the full ability range, so that different students could have anything from one word to a couple of sentences circled.

Indicating improvement
A symbol, such as an arrow, is used to indicate precisely where on the work improvement could be made (again avoiding written comment).

Giving an improvement suggestion
An improvement suggestion is written/asked for by the teacher, at the end of the work, to help the student know how to make the specific improvement.

3. Students make their improvement

Homework or class time (the beginning of the next lesson) is given for students to read the successes and improvement suggestion and to make their improvement (typical total maximum time needed: 10 minutes). *This may well take longer in the early days as the teacher and students learn their way!!*

Effective improvement prompts

In analysing many examples of teachers' marking, there appear to be three types of improvement prompts: a *reminder prompt,* a *scaffolded prompt* and an *example prompt.*

The **reminder prompt** is simply a rather unhelpful reiteration of the learning objective, for example:

- *Say more about saturation* (learning objective: To understand saturation point).

- *Give more detail about the impact of his reign* (learning objective: To describe the impact of Henry VIII's reign on the lives of ordinary people).

- *Write a more interesting ending to this story* (learning objective: To develop an effective story ending).

- *Redo this multiplication problem* (learning objective: To solve multiplication problems).

The **scaffolded prompt** involves the teacher giving examples and ideas as words or phrases, for example:

- *Say more about saturation. How much salt was used? How did you know saturation had been reached? When exactly was it reached?*

- *Give more detail. For instance: What else did he change? What kinds of people were affected by this change? In what ways did this affect them?*

- *Could you make your story more interesting? What did the character learn from his experiences? What advice might he give to future travellers?*

- *Redo this problem. You could use . . . method or . . . method.*

The **example prompt** involves the teacher giving exact models of what the student might write. The student is invited to choose one of these or to then write their own example.

Alternative ways of giving improvement suggestions

Once students understand the significance and the purpose of circling or highlighting successes and improvements, they rarely object to the apparent 'defacing' of their work. In fact, they want to know where their successes are if they don't appear! However, when the work is to be displayed as fair copy, clearly the piece should remain unblemished.

The Suffolk LEA guidance on marking suggests that with ongoing, more complex pieces of work, some teachers have used 'Post-it' notes or 'wrap-arounds'. Students keep the Post-it notes on the back page of their books. Some schools use Post-it notes with response partners (i.e. students read their partner's work and then say on a Post-it note two ways they could improve it). Alternatively, write feedback in pencil, so that students can rub it out after improvements have been made.

Examples of work marked by comment-only (by teacher)

Simon Butler, a teacher trialling this approach, modified the prompt sheet for teachers in the history department of his school (Fig. 5.1). Two examples of student work are then shown in Figures 5.2 and 5.3, illustrating how they were challenged and how they re-evaluated their work as a result of the feedback.

Fig. 5.1

Phase 1

At the very beginning of new work/assignment/enquiry explain to the class that you will be changing the way you will mark their written work in order to help them make more progress in the future.

Phase 2

Read all of the student's written work through very carefully <u>before</u> making any annotation. Next highlight three places in the writing where the student best met the learning intention(s) of the activity. Then indicate with a star where an improvement can be made to the original work.

Phase 3

Draw an arrow to a suitable space near the star and write a 'close the gap' prompt to support the student in making an improvement to their work. This can be provided in a variety of different forms:

Reminder prompt

most suitable for higher attaining students.

e.g. Say more about ....

e.g. Explain why you think this ....

e,g, An unfinished sentence – William showed he was a skillful battlefield commander when he ......

Example prompt

particularly supportive of lower attaining students.

e.g. Choose one of these statements and/or create your own.

Harold was unlucky because he had fought another battle against Norwegians

<u>Or</u>

Harold had a lot of bad luck particularly having to fight William soon after the Battle of Stamford Bridge.

Scaffold prompt

suitable for most students as it provides more structure to improve the work.

e.g. A Question – Can you explain why Harold's army were tired?

e.g. A Directive – Describe some of the preparations made by William which show that he was well organised.

Phase 4

Ensure that you provide time in class to enable students to read <u>and</u> respond to the 'close the gap' comment. This could also provide a suitable time to follow up individual needs with specific students 'face to face'. Finally, remember to comment upon their improvement at the first available opportunity.

Fig. 5.2

Why Did The Normans Win The Battle of Hastings?

When Edward the Confessor died in 1066 he left no heir to the throne. Three people all wanted to become King. In the end William won the battle. In this essay I will tell you why. The paragraphs shall be:

- Bad Luck
- Leadership skills
- William's personality
- Conclusion

Harold's bad luck was one of the reasons why William won the Battle of Hastings. Here are some examples. William was already annoyed with Harold for escaping his imprisonment, so he was even more determined to win. Harold and his troops also had to fight two battles in 17 days. One at Stamford Bridge and the other at Hastings, His troops were already tired before they met William at Hastings. Lastly, Harold got shot in the eye and died – very unlucky!

William was a skilled and experienced military leader with excellent tactical knowledge. Some historians believe that William deliberately made his army retreat, so that Harold's army would break their strong shield. While Harold's army were chasing them they regrouped and killed them all. This was all William's idea. **His infantry soldiers were highly trained and the cavalry rode specially bred horses. The soldiers were also equipped with chain mail armour to give them protection in battle.**

William was a wise man (and great man but took money from people for no reason, apart from the fact he had a greed for wealth. He supported the Pope and was kind to the people who were Christians. However he could be ruthless towards people who did not believe in God. William was very stern and put anyone in prison that acted against the law. He stopped houses being built over woodland for William loved nature his favourite animal was the tall stags.)

There are many reasons why William won The Battle of Hastings. However, I believe that if Harold's army had been fresh at the Battle of Hastings he would have had a much better chance of winning and becoming king. I also think Harold should have won because he was related to Edward the Confessor, he was an important Englishman. Whereas William only supported the Pope and was a good Soldier.

Feedback

Anne - A well structured answer with a topic sentence to start most paragraphs - you explained clearly why Harold's army were at a disadvantage at Hastings. You also presented your own opinion in the conclusion - well done

Target - This paragraph needs to be linked more closely to the question - the words underlined in black are probably not needed. Anne could you try to finish this sentence please. Then add some evidence from the previous paragraph.

e.g. William was a wise and determined man who carefully planned his attempt to ....

Student response

.......claim the throne of England. He took great care over his invasion preparations. He made sure his army was well equiped with chain mail, good horses and plenty of food.

Fig. 5.3

Why did William win the Battle of Hastings

William won the Battle of Hastings because he was better prepered and he waited for the writ time.

First Harold Godwinsons Army was attacked by Hardrada. Then Godwinson came back for more and killed Hardrada. Then He went to Hastings with no rest to fight the Normans.

The Norman Army were ready for war. And Harold came to the top of the hill. William ran up the Hill with all is might but he was pushed down. He used the retreat trick. He ran away the English chased him surounded him he turned and shot Godwinson in the eye and he died.

Feedback

Jason – A big point to start off your answer clearly focusing on the question – Yes this was indeed very important in helping William win the battle – the retreat trick was a very clever tactic in the battle – well identified.

Target – Jason it would be really useful to add a conclusion to this answer. Which of these two examples do you prefer or can you write your own ?

Example 1 – The main reason William won was because poor Harold had to fight two battles in a short space of time.

Example 2 – I think William won for lots of different reasons. However I think the most significant factor was his skilful leadership during the battle.

Your Idea –

Student response

In fact I think that Harold bad luck plus the tricks william used in the battle both were the same importance.

Fig. 5.4 Learning objective: To use a range of sources and contextual knowledge (World War 1)

Some very good research here and you give

lots of detail

Upbury Manor School

Assessment of Progress | X | 1 | 2 | 3 | 4 | 5 |

Comment/Target

NC/GCSE

* (1) Explain what you mean about being tricked

We were tricked by the government using their posters the whole lot is a lie, they said it would be fun and a bit bad, but it isn't fun at all, they said we owe going to war to our king and country, but we don't deserve this, and these terrible conditions

* (2) Explain how all this makes you feel

These conditions make you feel terrible, one minute you could be alive, the next dead or have a pain and slow death by the diseases. I'm not surprised that I heard someone who had trench fever ran in to no-mans land to let him die quickly without the un-thinkable pain. You start to think how lucky you are when you hear the screams and crys for the soldiers and you can tell the pain they are suffering!

Figures 5.4–5.7 show further examples of teacher marking against the learning objective and success criteria of the task, with the student's subsequent improvement.

Fig. 5.5 Learning objective: To write a complete story (test – given a title)

You're in Charge!

Hi. I'm Joshua and I want to tell you a story about my post job. It was terrible. I was seventeen, but I loved to earn money and I still do. It was just my nature.

It was the twenty-third of August, 1990. I had just got a job at McDonalds. My boss was called Ben, he wasn't the nicest man alive. But this particular day he had a meeting and for some strange reason he came up to me and said "I'm leaving you in charge of the kitchen for a while."

I was half worried and half delighted. I was in charge of people older than me! I started cooking some burgers but I didn't see the towel that a cook had left there so the cooker lit on fire while the burgers were on top.

I ran out of the kitchen looking for the fire extinguisher. I found it and carried it into the kitchen. I pressed it to turn it on and nothing happened. So I stepped out of the kitchen and all I could do was watch it burn.

Suddenly, Ben stepped in the door my stomach felt like it had been twisted. "WHAT! JOSHUA YOU'RE FIRED!!!" shouted Ben. I was glad to be out in the end.

So that's my story, it's not really my fault is it. I didn't break the towel on the cooker and I didn't break the fire..... Oh never mind. That's the end anyway. "Bye."

(continued)

Would you improve your ending. If you think seriously about the ending I'm sure you could make the final paragraph much more interesting - perhaps with a warning to other people - what did you learn?

* So was the point of that? Its what im hearing all over the place. There's a few all to do with fire safety. First, is that you should never leave a towell on a cooker, secondly, look around before you turn on oven on and finally always have a working fire extinguisher in a room. So there you have it I could have sued but I just went home and cried like a girl.

Fig. 5.6 Learning objective: To write an opening paragraph which introduces a problem and uses contrasts (video stimulus)

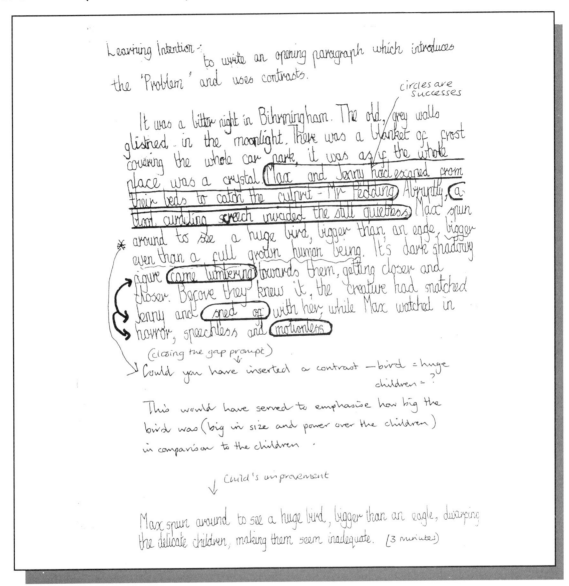

**Fig. 5.7 Learning objective:
To draw concise conclusions
reflecting the results
(Newtons of *force*)**

Learning Intention -:

To draw concise conclusions reflecting the results.

3 successes

Conclusion -: I found out that the harder you hit the drum the louder the sound and the softer you hit the drum the quieter the sound. I found out that the further the Newtons of force hitting the drum the louder the volume and the closer the Newtons of force hitting the drum the quieter the volume.

I found out that the drum moved slightly which could have effected our results. I found out that to make a fair test you need to have the same person to hit the drum and the same person to hold the sound meter in the same place.

I found out that the only variable we can change is the (volume) force we hit the drum with as we are testing the effect of this variable only.

closing the gap prompt

Thomas although you have described the overall trend you need to consider whether all the results follow the pattern. Do they? Why do you think you may have got these results?

Child's improvement

Learning Intention -:

To draw concise conclusions.

The final 2 results don't actually follow the pattern of a gradual overall increase. When I looked at the results of the trials I noticed that the results for trials 1,2,3 did not increase as much as they should. This might have been because when we moved the sound meter away from the drum we were changing more than 1 variable. Not only were we testing how the force we hit the drum affected the volume but also how distance can affect the volume.

(5 minutes)

Using the strategy orally

Improvement prompts of this type can of course be given to students orally within the context of practical ongoing work, during the course of a lesson. Pointing out successes before making improvement suggestions is vital. Making sure the focus is the learning objective of the task transforms unclear general suggestions into helpful specifics.

The impact of the success and improvement comment-only strategy

Many schools have had enormous success in using this strategy. Teachers in these schools have discovered marking to be a more meaningful and focused process. Before experimenting with comment-only marking, it can be useful to interview a random group of students about their views on the current marking in the school, then repeat the same interview at the end of a trial period. Often teachers from different departments are sceptical about new ideas. Nothing is more convincing than proof that it works for the students in their school. A small group of teachers, from Upbury Manor Art College in Medway, trialled this way of marking and were able to convincingly share their findings with the rest of the staff by first showing them the students' 'before and after' views. Quotes from the group of mixed-ability Years 7–9 students from the school include:

Before

Sometimes we don't know what our grades are actually for.

If I get a 'good' I don't often know what I've done good.

It would be good if teachers wrote how you could improve your work more.

Comments are better than grades.

Teachers expect you to know what they mean in comments.

Teachers sometimes rush you to do work so you don't really understand it.

After

You wouldn't know what you were doing without the learning objective.

My teachers write really long comments now about my work – and I understand them.

We have to correct our own work now, but it's easier now we have proper comments to help us.

Comments in my book help me improve my work and get a higher grade next time – that's new.

Teachers should test us at the end of the lesson to check that we've really understood the learning objective.

(continued)

Before	After
If I don't understand a comment in my book, I don't ask. It's too embarrassing.	*Learning objectives are good when you are revising because they sum up what the work was about.*
I get 'try harder' a lot, but it doesn't really help me do any better.	*If a teacher wrote 'try harder' in my book now I'd ask them how.*
I can't be bothered to correct my work, but if the teacher asked us to then I would.	*Sometimes I forget what it is I have to do – so I read the learning objective and then I know.*
When teachers ring your mistakes you can't see what the mistakes was.	

(b) Targets over a period of time

At regular intervals, usually at the end of a unit of work, quality comment-only marking needs to suggest long-term improvement suggestions. These act as a summary for students of where they are in relation to levels and overall achievement, and suggest explicit ways forward. A variety of approaches can help students meet these targets, but of prime importance is *(a)* the active role of the student in helping to determine, track and judge the success of their targets, and *(b)* the provision of strategies which help the student to know *how* to progress.

Self-, paired and group judging of work against test criteria (anonymous and their own) and against exemplars of sample answers, especially where varying quality is exemplified, enables students to analyse work critically and objectively and motivates them to take control over their own progress. Students need to know explicitly what would make the difference between, say, Level 5 and Level 6. Without this knowledge, they are simply guessing at how to get a higher grade.

Various useful examples of effective target setting from *Good Assessment in Secondary Schools* from OFSTED (2003) include:

 The following are characteristics common to the effective setting of targets in all subjects. The targets are:

- *specific to the subject and relate to important aspects of knowledge, understanding and skills in that subject;*

- *derived from teachers' assessments and not only student devised;*

- *limited in number and of manageable proportions;*

■ *relatively short-term, capable of being monitored and subject to regular amendment;*

■ *stored so that they are accessible to the students as they undertake the next task (for example, in a planner or draft book), not locked in a cabinet;*

■ *drawn from, or relate to, the teaching objectives of a unit of work or the assessment criteria for the current task, and so are immediately relevant and can be referred to in marking and feedback.* ❜

Some examples of teacher comments on History scripts relating to ongoing targets:

❛ *An excellent answer as far as it goes – but it does not mention sources. If it did this, it would be Level 4 against the examiner's mark scheme, but without the sources it can only be level 2.* ❜

❛ *Good. You have shown how to link points. This will get you higher grades in the exam if you can explain yourself in this way.* ❜

A comment, given for coursework (an application), is shown here. The subject is design and technology and the task was related to the design and fixing of a desk leg:

❛ *Your sketching shows good ability to record shape and form identifying crucial features. Good comparisons made between cast aluminium and fabricated steel.*

Target: *broaden the range of solutions: can the leg/frame joint be achieved without a bracket, or without using metal? Look at frame construction in architecture.* ❜

Another example describes the organisation of a lesson in which students determined their own targets and, in doing so, made links across other subjects:

❛ *Year 11 students at Withernsea High School and Technology College enjoyed a history lesson that reviewed recent examination scripts. The lesson concentrated on how marks had been awarded in the light of the mark scheme. The teacher, with the aid of an overhead projector, asked students to apply the mark scheme to exemplar answers. Using mini-whiteboards, students held up the marks they gave for each answer, following general and paired discussion about application of the marking criteria. The teacher ensured that there was a representative range of examples. The students were asked to consider how their own work could be enhanced by what they were doing.*

'Time was taken to explore the application of each level in the mark scheme and the students rapidly gained in confidence and understanding. The work moved them forward in their thinking about specific learning targets that would improve their own examination performance. In discussing what they had gained from this lesson, the two students (interviewed) were clear about what they needed to do to improve their own work in history but also felt that the ideas had relevance for their work in English. They were able to link what they had learned to the requirement to interpret two short story writers' choice of language in describing characters and story settings. They recognised that they needed to improve their skills in the quick scanning of a text, but that the history work would help them make selections of texts for comparison and interpretation, and sharpened their awareness of the demands of particular questions. **,**

(OFSTED, 2003)

Levels Review Week

Some schools organise a 'Levels review week', in which the timetable is organised so that ongoing teacher/student conferences take place. The subject of discussion is basically what has been achieved and what the student needs to try to achieve by the end of the year or the next conference. The teacher's role is to help the student know or find out how to meet these aims. Such interviews can be a waste of time if there is no carefully planned and agreed structure to the process.

Once targets are successfully tracked by students, the meetings tend to run themselves: the discussion is about the student demonstrating where she or he believes they have now met their targets and suggesting what they now need to focus on. In order for new targets to be suggested, the student will need permanent access to the exam or next-up level criteria and the teacher will need to have looked at the student's work in order to contribute suggestions. Students find such individual specific attention to needs welcome and motivating.

One School's approach to success and improvement marking

The following account presents a number of solutions to some of the problems and issues discussed so far. Teachers from the history department from Upbury Arts College in Medway wanted to:

■ be selective about coverage: focusing on key skills and progression;

■ find a way to do quality success and improvement marking on key pieces of work;

■ make learning a priority;

■ enable students to be central in the learning process.

The approach they trialled had very successful results, fulfilling all their aims and more.

Upbury Arts College: told by Sally Fisher

In much the same way that students can easily lose sight of the bigger picture in the absence of learning signposts, teachers too are in danger of this if learning objectives do not connect with previous and next-step learning. A succession of unrelated learning outcomes will fragment learning because they won't, on their own, lead anywhere. Teachers, and students, need to be clear where each learning objective used is heading in terms of overall learning. A possible structure would be one which works from outcomes back to objectives, to enable teachers to see how the various learning objectives and success criteria work together. The structure we used is outlined in Fig. 5.8.

As a subject department, decide to 'quality mark' (i.e. comment only: looking for success and improvement needs) only four pieces of work a term. This needs eventually to become school policy. These are called Key Challenges 1/2/3/4.

Step 1

Steps involved	Example in action
Take a Scheme of Work (a term in length) and identify the four key challenges for that term.	■ The History Department initially went through a Year 7 Autumn Term SoW on the Roman Empire (Fig. 5.9). ■ We drew up a table listing the Learning Objectives on the left-hand side and the skills needed to meet each objective on the right (Fig. 5.10). ■ We then focused on the right hand side of the table ('Skills Needed') and highlighted recurring skills / where skills linked and

(continued)

opportunities for consolidation and progression. Where such opportunities were not apparent, we built them in.

■ We then had a clearer idea of what the main learning focus was for the SoW. We then identified the four key pieces of work and these were justified in terms of learning objectives, rather than because we particularly 'loved teaching that bit'. It was also important that we offered a range of learning activities too (Fig. 5.11).

Step 2

Highlight these four Key Challenges. Now discuss the following:

■ Are there any skills/links between them?
■ Is there progression?
■ Where will the students have opportunities to practise any targets arising from each Key Challenge? *If the opportunity isn't apparent, it needs to be built into the Scheme of Work.*

Prune parts of the Scheme of Work which do not contribute directly to the Key Challenges.

Once the four key pieces of work had been identified, we had to reorder the SoW to ensure we could build in skill progression. Then we began pruning. We took out anything which did not directly contribute to the key pieces.

Step 3

■ Take the first Key Challenge and discuss what the students will need to be able to do, in order to succeed in this piece of work.
■ Work backwards now to identify what the learning objectives and success criteria need to be for the lessons leading up to this key challenge (i.e. *What do I need the students to learn?, What will they need to do* (process) *in order to meet that learning?*)
■ We then took each Key Challenge in turn and worked backwards. We discussed what students would need to be able to do (what learning they required) in order to succeed in each Key Challenge. These informed what the learning objectives and success criteria leading up to each piece of work were (Fig. 5.12).
■ You will note on Fig. 5.12 (bottom left) *'religion ????'*. This indicates how we initially worked. In order for our students to succeed/practise the skills for Key Challenge 3, we knew that they needed to be practise the skill of 'selecting and combining information'. We decided that this would come from a focus on Roman religion but we needed to work out the detail. This is an important example because it illustrates our absolute focus on skills progression. We were using only the parts of the original SoW which served the learning.
■ Fig. 5.13 outlines some of the methods which could be used to formatively mark those key pieces.

The impact of this way of working
■ It puts student involvement in the learning process at its heart.

(continued)

- It puts the learning process at the heart of classroom teaching.
- This method has ensured that formative assessment does not become a 'bolt on' or stand-alone 'initiative', but is integral to all learning.
- It prevents the sharing of learning objectives and success criteria from becoming formulaic and mechanical in their use by teachers and by students.
- This approach provides a rationale for learning objectives and success criteria for teachers. They are less likely to lose sight of the bigger learning picture or neglect sharing learning objectives and success criteria because there is an understanding of the importance of these as building blocks to key pieces of work.
- There is no longer the blind panic about having to race through everything in the curriculum, because the key areas of learning have already been identified and so the selection process has already been decided by the Department. The Department has used its professional judgment to decide what it is that students really need to know, and has been able to justify the key pieces in terms of the learning aims they serve. For teachers, this very process has been incredibly empowering and liberating.
- This approach frees up time to really drive home *understanding* rather than simply plough on through the coverage amid a sea of confused faces. A personal example I used when I did some training on this: I have vivid memories of not being able 'to do' fractions at primary school and left at eleven still not being able 'to do' them. When I encountered more challenging fraction work at secondary school, I couldn't do it then either (hardly surprising). So I left school with the belief that fractions were something that I simply couldn't do. Of course that wasn't true at all. The truth is that no one had planned for my not understanding. The approach I suggest above plans to ensure that skills, etc, are revisited **within** a unit of work to ensure that learning is consolidated. There is no point simply testing the skills at the end of the unit when you then don't have time to deal with any gaps in understanding revealed by the test. (More of this in the next chapter.)

Looking at a Scheme of Work as a whole rather than in lesson chunks, as this approach suggests, forces teachers to map student learning far more effectively. Many teachers I have worked with using this process have been staggered by the lack of progression demanded within their Scheme of Work. Indeed, quite often **less** was expected of the students as they actually progressed **through** units. Clear building-blocks for learning have to be signposted. As any PE teacher would tell us: you can't teach a somersault until you've taught forward rolls. The process of actually identifying what the four Key Challenges are to be requires planners to look for links in skills. At this stage the progression within a Scheme of Work, in terms of skills, should be evident. However, this progression won't simply happen by itself or by virtue of it being highlighted on a Scheme of Work. In order for the students to make these jumps in their understanding and learning, the progression needs to be clearly planned. The learning objectives and success criteria you use are the blocks on which to build the learning and to ensure the progression. This method has had quite a powerful effect on teachers. They now have a much sharper focus on not only what the learning should be, but also on where the learning is going. Because this is shared with the students, there is a certain 'moving forward together' spirit.

(continued)

Fig. 5.8

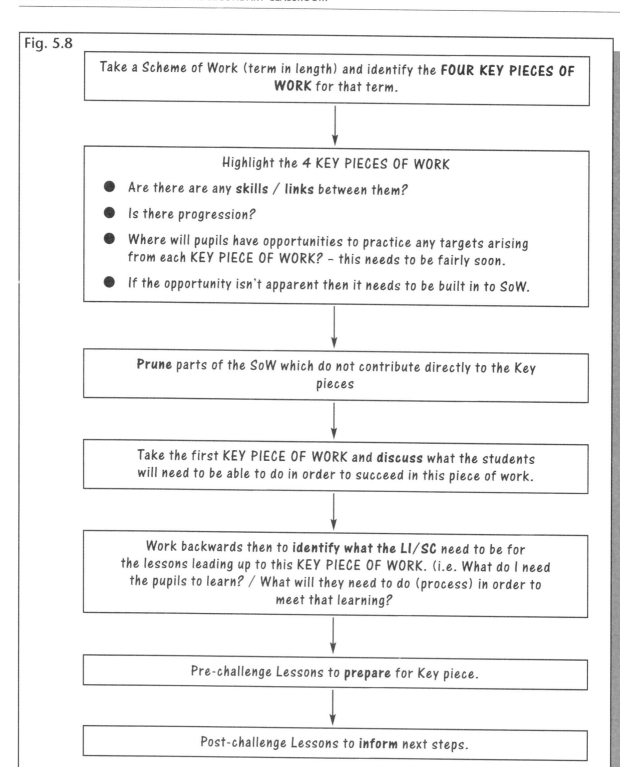

(continued)

Fig. 5.9

Study Unit: The Roman Empire
Focus: How did the Romans build their empire?
Organising idea: WHY DID THE ROMANS BUILD THEIR EMPIRE?
HOW SUCCESSFUL WAS THE ROMAN ARMY?

Learning Intention	Activities and routes	LS	Success Criteria	Notes
To write a persuasive letter	Core: Pair work on reasons for / against invasion Whole group discussion. Discuss SC. Pupils draft letter. Pupils write up after proof reading. 3-4-5 activity. Read yellow booklets. Pupils play Army game – discuss their experiences. Explain choice of task (handbook/diary entry/TV doc./ cartoon strip) to present life of R. soldier. Mastery Learning test. Reinforcement: Use diff sheet. Can cut & move reasons into order. Use writing frame. Can use writing framed booklets.		Explain some of the disadvan and explain some of the adva Use persuasive words from the list Make your own opinion clear in your conclusion	
To practise proof reading our work			Correct key spellings, capital letters and full stops.	
To learn about how the Roman army was organised	G and T: use diff map sheet (more detailed). Should use sheet outlining problems facing Cl. in their letter. Research in more detail using range of texts. H/W: Draft work / proof reading / self evaluation / devise own fact or opinion exercise/ Internet research (see below)		Give at least 2 examples under each heading to show how the army was organised Explain how some of these examples made the army so successful	
To examine the life of a Roman soldier	ICT: Cut and paste evidence to table / Use writing frame / word process letter Research : www.ancientsites.com/xi/places/ Home./index.rage?loc=Rome See BBC online – good for lower ability pupils		Research information about R. soldiers Present this information in an organised way.	

(continued)

Fig. 5.10

The Roman Empire

Learning Intention	Skills Needed
1. To write a summary of a story	Picking out the key elements of a story
2. To understand what the words "fact" and "myth" actually mean.	Compare fact and myth using evidence to support conclusions.
3. To weigh up the disadvantages and advantages of types of Roman Government.	Knowledge. Description and explanation. Supported judgements.
4. To write a persuasive letter	Persuasive language. Description and explanation. Supported judgements.
5. To practice proof reading work.	Key words and grammar.
6. To learn about how the Roman Army was organised.	Note taking. Explanation and supported judgements.
7. To examine the life of a Roman soldier.	Research. Organisation of information. Presentation. Persuasive writing.
8. To compare life in Britain before and after the Roman Invasion.	Knowledge, explanation. Comparison and supported description.
9. To write a persuasive and informative account.	Research. Organisation of information. Key words. Presentation. Persuasive writing, propaganda.
10. To understand what is meant by religious intolerance.	Knowledge and understanding. Comparison. Source work, selection and identification of information.
11. To examine why Christianity became accepted into the Roman Empire.	Cause and Consequence. Supported judgements.
12. To understand how the Roman Empire declined.	Cause and consequence. Linking causes and consequences. Judgements.
13. To examine the legacy of the Roman Empire.	Knowledge and understanding. Cause and consequence.

(continued)

Fig. 5.11

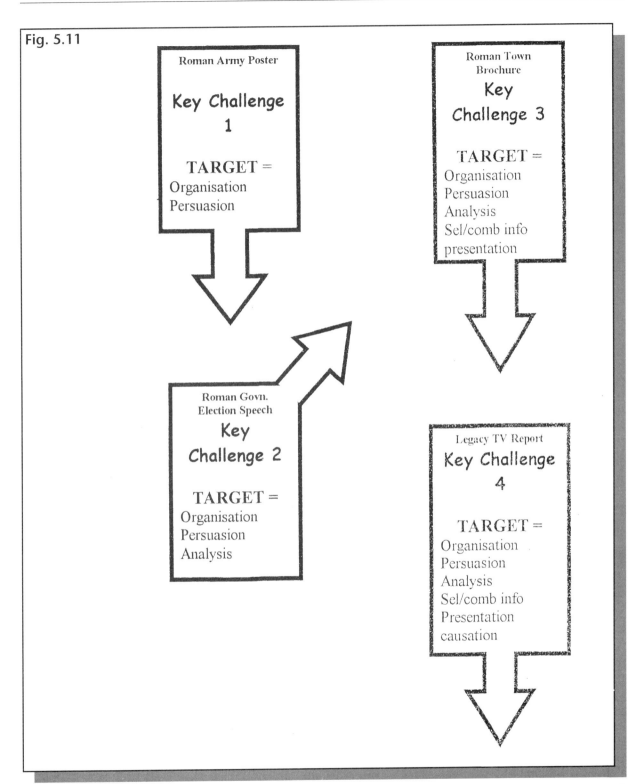

(continued)

Fig. 5.12

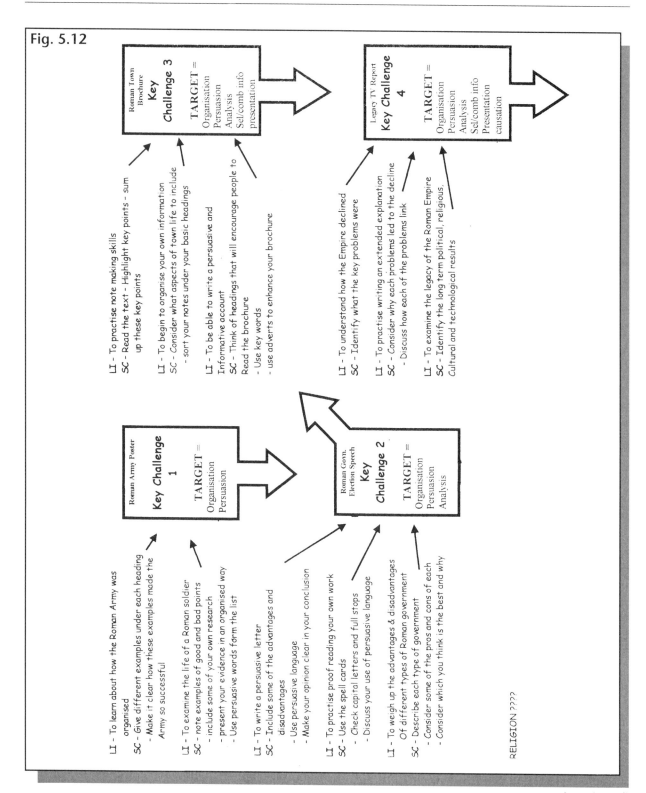

(continued)

Fig. 5.13

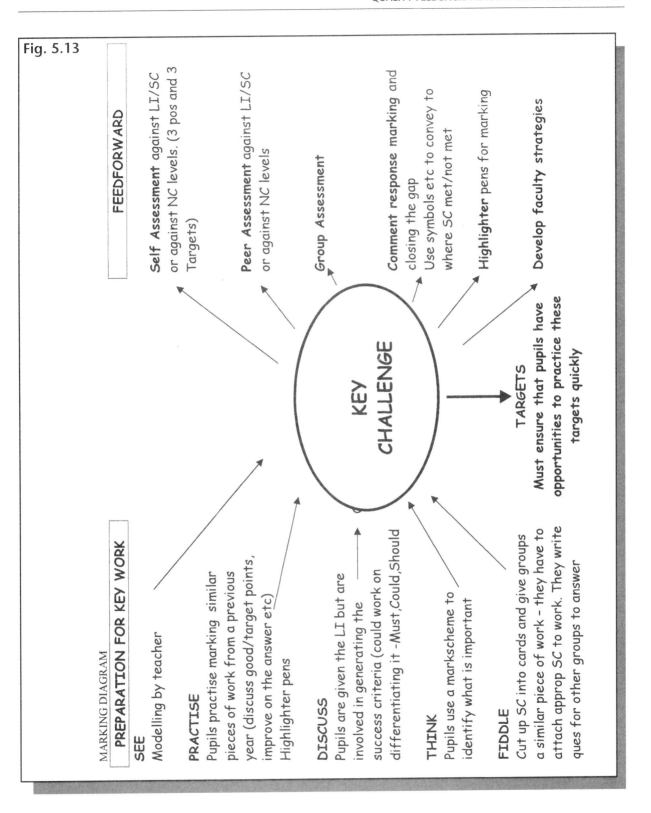

MARKING DIAGRAM

PREPARATION FOR KEY WORK

SEE
Modelling by teacher

PRACTISE
Pupils practise marking similar pieces of work from a previous year (discuss good/target points, improve on the answer etc)
Highlighter pens

DISCUSS
Pupils are given the LI but are involved in generating the success criteria (could work on differentiating it -Must,Could,Should

THINK
Pupils use a markscheme to identify what is important

FIDDLE
Cut up SC into cards and give groups a similar piece of work – they have to attach approp SC to work. They write ques for other groups to answer

KEY CHALLENGE

FEEDFORWARD

Self Assessment against LI/SC or against NC levels. (3 pos and 3 Targets)

Peer Assessment against LI/SC or against NC levels

Group Assessment

Comment response marking and closing the gap
Use symbols etc to convey to where SC met/not met

Highlighter pens for marking

Develop faculty strategies

TARGETS
Must ensure that pupils have opportunities to practice these targets quickly

Key principles

- Marking is one aspect of a wider feedback policy.

- Comment-only feedback leads to higher learning gains than grades alone or grades with comments.

- Focusing feedback (oral or written) on success and improvement needs against the learning objective of the task leads to students embedding their improvements and applying them in subsequent work.

- Students need time to make improvements on their work.

- Improvement should focus on either:

  (a) short-term improvement on the work marked, or
  (b) longer-term targets.

- Teachers should model feedback processes aiming for maximum student control over marking.

INSET ideas

1. Introduce teachers to the success and improvement model, stressing that they would only mark occasional pieces in this way (once a week, twice at the most). Show some of the examples in this chapter.
2. Use the same piece of a student's writing for a whole staff to mark using the strategy. Get people to share their improvement suggestions. Encourage them to go beyond a reminder prompt.
3. At a subsequent meeting, teachers can bring students' work and have a go at the strategy in pairs, again working on improvement suggestions together.
4. Teachers bring along to the next meeting the students' work, now complete with improvements, discuss and analyse the relationship between the quality of the improvement prompt and the quality of the improvement then made.
5. Teachers trial the ideas suggested for involving students in assessing against test criteria.
6. Discuss strategies outlined for student reviews, building on and analysing existing practice.
7. After time, review the current marking policy in the light of staff trialling.

6 Self- and peer assessment

> Independent learners have the ability to seek out and gain new skills, new knowledge and new understandings. They are able to engage in self-reflection and to identify the next steps in their learning. Teachers should equip learners with the desire and the capacity to take charge of their learning through developing the skills of self-assessment.
>
> *(Assessment Reform Group, 2002)*

Our aim is, of course, to involve students as far as possible in the analysis and constructive criticism of their own work. If the teacher is the only person giving feedback, the balance is wrong and the students become powerless, with no stake in their learning. What is more, marking is, in those circumstances, time-consuming, unwieldy and 'end-on'.

We want students to use self-evaluation continually, so that reflection, pride in successes, modification and improvement become a natural part of the process of learning. Once trained to be able to identify success against the success criteria of a task, students can relatively easily identify their own and each other's successes. With all subjects, students can also, given the criteria and good models of excellence, make their own improvements, albeit with input from the teacher at some stage.

Self-assessment

Quality self-assessment is clearly very powerful, but to be successful often needs a gradual training programme and ground rules to be set. If students are let loose on their own or each other's work too soon, they will head mercilessly for the spelling errors or make stinging remarks about the quality of the handwriting or work in general.

A common first stage of shifting power from teacher to student is to get students to mark their own work. Paired marking involves the emotional dynamic between two students, so is often tackled after students are confident about reflecting on their own work first. The current ethos of the classroom determines the significance of this order.

Examples of enabling self-assessment

(a) Shifting power from teacher to student with the 'success and improvement' marking strategy

Three stages tend to be most commonly followed by teachers to enable students to independently assess and mark their own and each other's work, using the 'success and improvement' marking strategy. Clearly, the age of the students would determine how much time would need to be spent at each stage. The stages are intended to relate to students marking their own work or marking each other's work together.

Either within lessons, during homework time or at the beginning of the next lesson:

Stage 1: students identify their own successes
Teachers using the success and improvement model have found that students can easily identify their own successes if the learning objective is clear (a knowledge, skill or concept, rather than a broad application) by circling or highlighting. During class time, these can then be read to the person next to them or shared in a group or whole-class setting. The positive influence of identifying successes has a great impact on students' self-esteem and motivation to continue to improve their work.

Stage 2: students identify a place for improvement
Once the finding of successes is established, students can be asked – after they have been working for some time, if in lesson time, or on their own if homework – to not only identify one or two successes, but also to find one place in their work which could be improved against the learning objective. One strategy is to ask students to identify this place by drawing a wiggly line underneath the sentence or phrase to be improved, ready for the teacher to write an improvement suggestion. The teacher then

writes the improvement suggestion for the student; the student then makes the improvement on the work when it is given back at the beginning of the next lesson.

Stage 3: students identify their successes and make an 'on the spot' improvement
Students can then be asked to identify an area to be improved and make the improvement as part of the lesson or at home. If this happens in class, it seems to work best if students do this first on their own, although, if they are used to paired discussion, they might well be able to launch headlong into paired discussion about the best ways of making the improvement. The teacher is then presented with work which not only has success identified by the student, but also improvements made at the time (usually evidenced by parts underlined then improved at the foot of the piece, or words or phrases crossed out and rewritten at the foot. Students should be encouraged to experiment where appropriate – e.g. with English writing, writing more than one possible improvement of a sentence or phrase (see Fig. 6.1).

Once this stage has been reached, the teacher's role changes from being a full-time 'marker' to an effective interventionist, commenting on students' efforts and getting involved in their decision-making.

(b) Use of success criteria

Once success criteria for lessons have been established, they present themselves as a natural vehicle for continual self-assessment. If students have copied the success criteria under the title of their work, they can then either tick off all the ingredients or steps on their finished work to show they have been fulfilled, or colour code each one and circle the various elements of the work at the end. When the success criteria are closed and have right or wrong answers, self-assessment is simply a yes/no exercise. When the success criteria deal with elements on a continuum of quality, as is often the case with skills such as persuading, summarising, comparing, characterising, debating, etc, self-assessment becomes focused around those success criteria which need improving. The student can say that each element has been included, but not necessarily know whether they are good examples. This is where peer-assessment and the use of exemplar modelling come into their own. The following pages give effective examples of both.

Fig. 6.1 Learning objective: To write an opening paragraph with contrasts

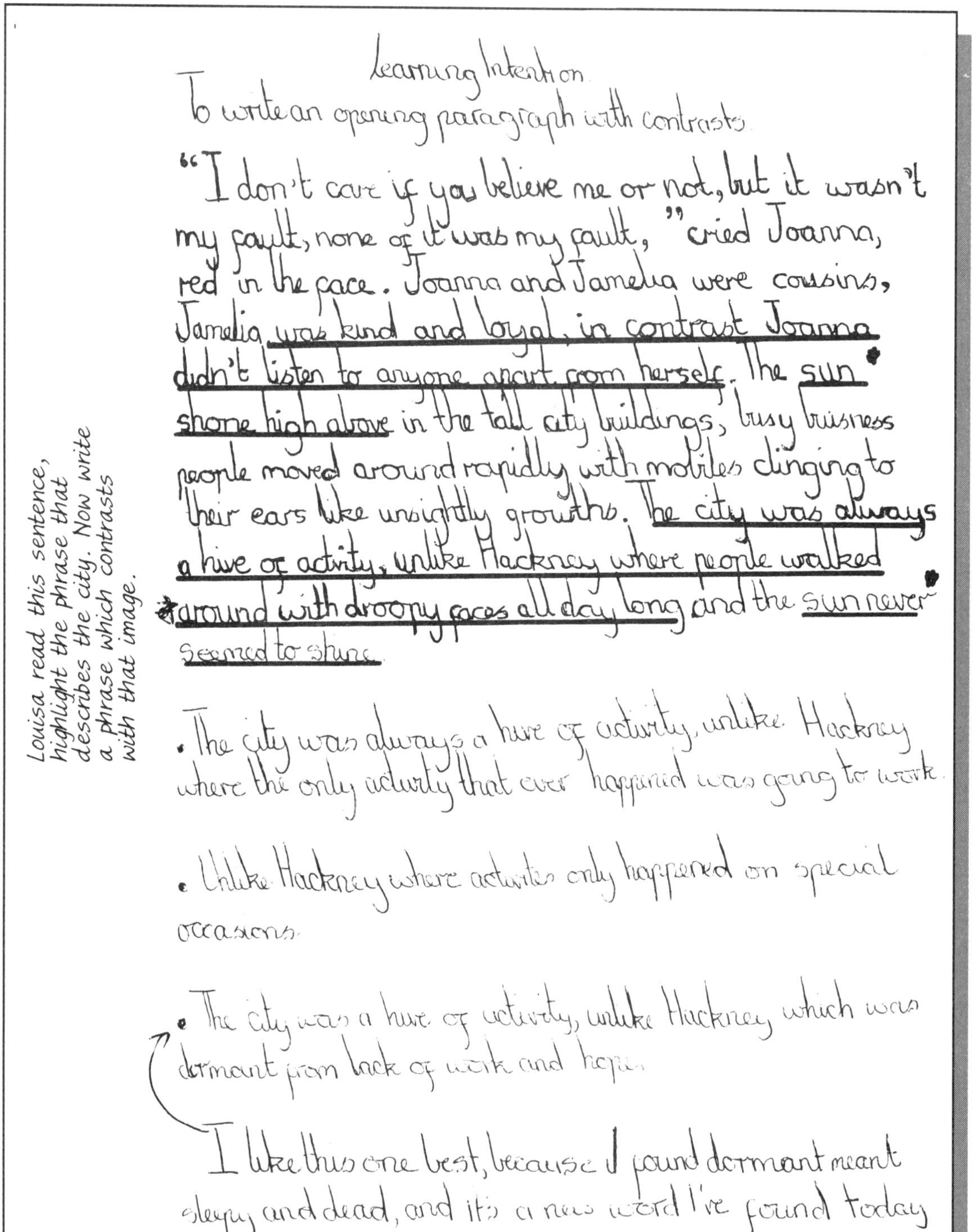

Learning Intention

To write an opening paragraph with contrasts.

"I don't care if you believe me or not, but it wasn't my fault, none of it was my fault," cried Joanna, red in the face. Joanna and Jamelia were cousins, Jamelia was kind and loyal, in contrast Joanna didn't listen to anyone apart from herself. The sun shone high above in the tall city buildings, busy business people moved around rapidly with mobiles clinging to their ears like unsightly growths. The city was always a hive of activity, unlike Hackney where people walked around with droopy faces all day long and the sun never seemed to shine.

Louisa read this sentence, highlight the phrase that describes the city. Now write a phrase which contrasts with that image.

• The city was always a hive of activity, unlike Hackney where the only activity that ever happened was going to work.

• Unlike Hackney where activities only happened on special occasions.

• The city was a hive of activity, unlike Hackney which was dormant from lack of work and hope.

I like this one best, because I found dormant meant sleepy and dead, and it's a new word I've found today

Fig. 6.2

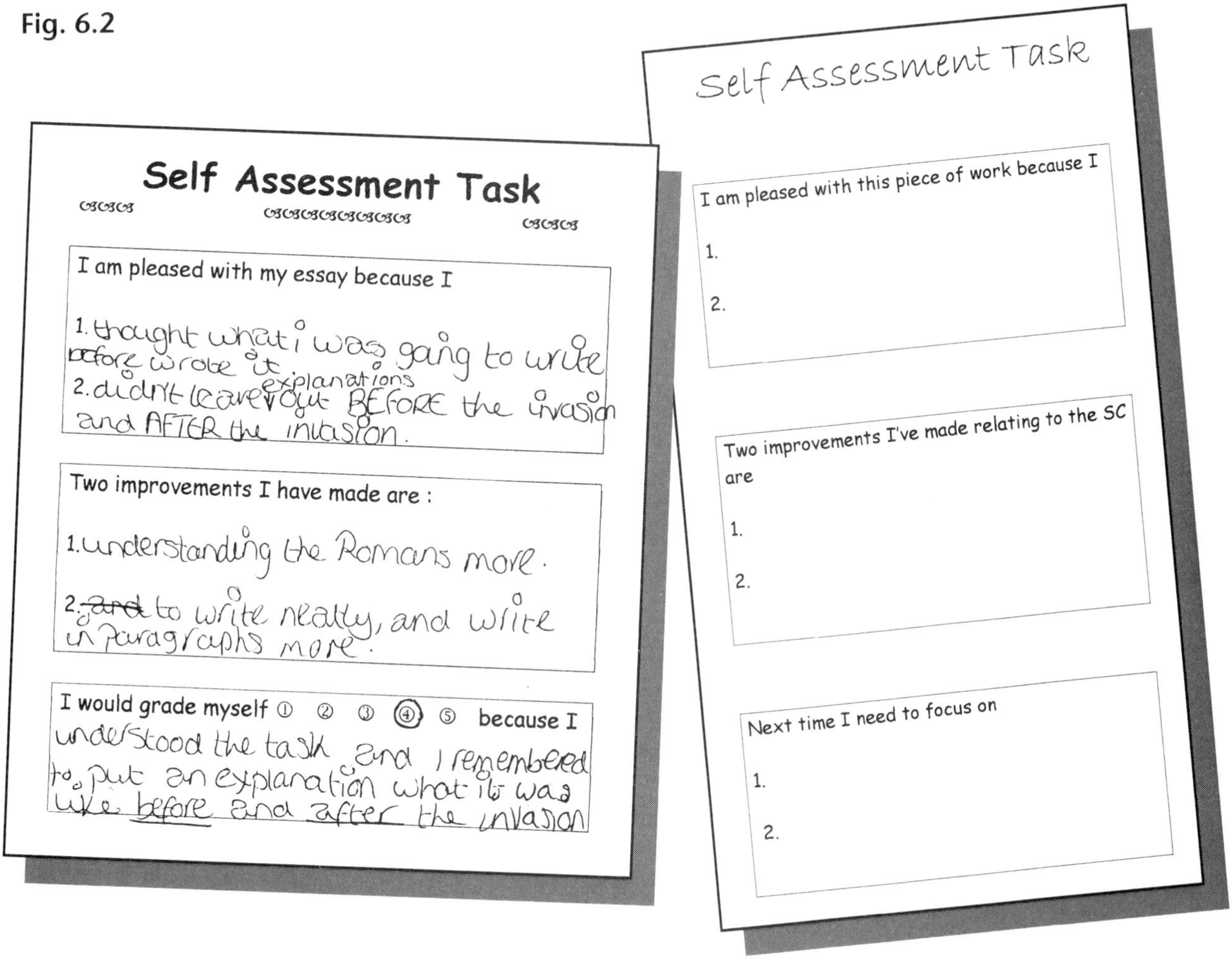

Self Assessment Task

I am pleased with my essay because I

1. thought what i was going to write before wrote it.
2. didn't leave out explanations BEFORE the invasion and AFTER the invasion.

Two improvements I have made are :

1. understanding the Romans more.
2. ~~and~~ to write neally, and write in paragraphs more.

I would grade myself ① ② ③ ④ ⑤ because I understood the task and I remembered to put an explanation what it was like before and after the invasion

Self Assessment Task

I am pleased with this piece of work because I

1.

2.

Two improvements I've made relating to the SC are

1.

2.

Next time I need to focus on

1.

2.

Figures 6.2, 6.3 and 6.4 are examples of templates for self-assessment created by Sally Fisher. Fig. 6.5 gives an example of a student colour-coding work against the success criteria.

The following example of self-assessment shows the importance of the specificity of the criteria involved and the modelling carried out to make the task and the content crystal-clear:

❛ *In a Year 7 geography lesson the teacher discussed a decision-making exercise from the previous lesson concerning the location of a leisure centre. He provided several alternative answers. Students were asked to rank these answers in terms of quality against the marking criteria. As a result, students were clearly able to see the difference between simple descriptions and attempts to explain and analyse the information. Students were then asked to compare their own answers with the*

Fig. 6.3

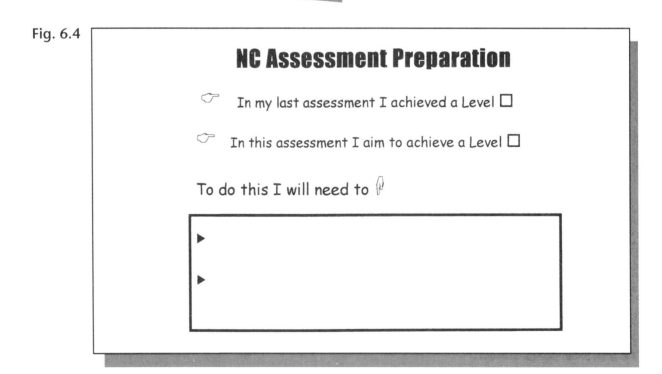

NC Assessment

I achieved a NC Level ____ because I :
1.

2.

In order to achieve a NC Level ____ I need
to :
1.

2.

NC Assessment

Where I met the SC –
I used 3 Paragraphs
used more than one Source
I used Persuasive language
I used Some of your own Ideas
I give Examples .

In order to improve my level I need to –
use more than One Source
i ~~ws~~ need to organise what
info goes where .

Fig. 6.4

NC Assessment Preparation

☞   In my last assessment I achieved a Level ☐

☞   In this assessment I aim to achieve a Level ☐

To do this I will need to ☞

▶

▶

Fig. 6.5

22nd May

to write a persuasive speech.
- use P.E.E.
- <u>include powerful words</u>
- make your opinion clear.

You should move to the town
because it's <u>fantastic</u>.
　　There are lots of jobs, lots of
houses and lots of shops. most
of the shops sell food example:
fish and bread. The fish and
bread are alot cheaper than the
village.
　　　　Building houses is one of the
main jobs in the town so more people
come to live here in this wonderful
town. Just like you, there is a couple of houses
just been built, maybe you should move
into one.
　　The town has lots of protection
like a wall round the whole town
to stop other people from coming in,
there are weapons such as
swords.←――― And lots more.
　　There is enough transport
for everyone in the town, you
could walk or even go in a cart.
　　Most of the houses are
made out of wood to stop them
from getting cold inside. Although
the other houses are made out
of straw the are no windows

(continued)

cheap↓

So you can buy covers and blankets from the stalls in the market.

Another reason why ~~i think~~ *you should move* to the town is because the is plenty of food and drink↗

for you to live on

The main tow things idid in the speech was P.E.E. and making my opinion clear but i, would need to put more powerful words in.

examples and decide which one of their answers had fitted best. The students were clearly inspired to analyse their own work, comparing it with a better answer and highlighting how their own could be improved. 🙶

(OFSTED, 2003)

(c) Use of traffic lights

For some time, teachers have experimented with 'traffic lights' as a way of getting students to rate their achievement (green for achieved, amber for half-achieved, red for not achieved: need help). I have some reservations about the use of traffic lights, having seen them mainly used by students at the end of a piece of work to indicate a judgement of their achievement. Over a number of years I have attempted to establish where they work well and where they can be detrimental to student self-efficacy. First of all, some of my concerns:

■ Coding at the end of a piece of work in this way can be crude and simplistic. Students who are over-confident tend to over-estimate their achievement. Similarly, less confident students tend to under-estimate their achievement.

■ The comparison effect is explicitly set up. At a glance, students can see how they appear to be doing compared to others.

■ If a student puts a red at the end of their work, this must be the fault of the teacher, not the student. Either the work was inappropriately modelled or was completely mismatched to the student's ability. The time to seek help is during the process of the lesson or while the work is being done. The end is too late! There may, of course, be exceptional circumstances where a student believed they knew what they were doing for homework, but at the time found it difficult.

■ With open skill success criteria (where there is no definite answer, but a continuum of quality) I have further problems. If I feel I have succeeded at three out of five success criteria really well, is that amber? What if I had achieved all five criteria but without much quality? How about if I met only two criteria but, in the case of English writing, wrote a more powerful piece than if I had attended to them all?

Paul Spenceley, from The Hundred of Hoo secondary school in Medway, uses traffic-lighting very successfully against the knowledge facts in his subject: science. This is where the system works well: with definitive knowledge facts rather than elements of achievement that can only be deemed to be of a particular standard when compared to a model exemplar. Traffic lights can also be used very effectively as a *starting point* for dialogue.

At the beginning of a unit of work his students are given a chart of science facts which they 'traffic-light' according to their present knowledge (see Fig. 6.6). At the end of the unit, they are asked to do the same thing in the next column. This establishes current understanding and gives students a clear idea of revision areas and/or where to seek assistance or clarification, leading to a student summary sheet (Fig. 6.7). Another effective use of traffic lights is given on page 125.

Fig. 6.6

	The Hundred of Hoo School - Science Faculty Key Stage Four **Title:** Human body – action and control – self assessment sheet	Unit 1	Level C/S
One Company		Lesson 1	Worksheet 1a

Use traffic lights to assess what you know now, and again at the end of this unit	Start	End
I know three things the mouth does to food.		
I know what the stomach does to food.		
I know what the small and large intestines each do to food.		
I understand how the small intestine is specially adapted to do its job.		
I know what the gall bladder and pancreas do in the digestive system.		
I understand about the three main types of enzymes and their jobs.		
I know what red cells, white cells and plasma each do in blood.		
I understand how a scab is formed when the body is cut.		
I know what a nerve cell looks like and why.		
I know how the eye adjusts the amount of light it allows in.		
I know how drugs affect the nervous system.		
I know other affects that drugs can have on the body and it's organs.		
I understand what homeostasis is and why it is important.		
I understand why body temperature and water levels in the body have to be controlled.		
I know the organs of the urinary system and their jobs.		
I know two or more jobs done by the kidney.		
I know the structure of skin, and what the parts of it do.		
I understand some ways in which the skin helps to control body temperature.		
I understand which things the skin senses and how it informs the brain.		

Your teacher will read through the table above and will give a little bit more detail about each of the sentences. You then need to decide how confident you are about your understanding **now**.

Colour the **start** box using these rules:

GREEN – sure you could explain this to other people.

ORANGE – can remember something about this, but not everything.

RED – do not understand this or have never heard of it.

Fig. 6.7

Traffic light summary sheet
AT2 – Biology

Section of KS3 work	colour	Details I would like to cover again or need some help understanding
Cells - structure and function e.g. muscle, sperm, ovum. Tissues and organs.		
Food, nutrition and digestion - healthy diet, enzymes and the need for energy from food.		
skeleton, joints and muscles (antagonistic pairs) in movement .		
Human reproduction and development of the fetus. Role of the placenta. Puberty.		
Lung structure and function - and the effects of smoking.		
Respiration releasing energy from food in plants *and* animals - including word equation.		
Health and drugs and bacteria and viruses. The immune system. Vaccination and medicines.		
Photosynthesis, light and minerals for healthy plants.		
Environmental and inherited causes of variation		
Selective breeding by man can lead to new varieties. E.g. cattle for milk or meat.		
Classifying living things - putting them into groups		
populations, predators and prey, competition for resources and adaptation to environments.		
Food chains, food webs and pyramids of numbers. Poisons in food chains.		

Peer assessment

The emotional impact of peer assessment

One of the reasons peer assessment is so valuable is because students often give and receive criticisms of their work more freely than in the traditional teacher/student interchange. Another advantage is that the language used by students to each other is the language they would naturally use, rather than 'school' language.

Peer assessment can involve a few minutes of students helping each other to improve their work, or a more lengthy process of reading whole pieces and analysing them more fully together.

In order to fully understand the emotional impact of sharing one's work with a peer and receiving criticism, no matter how constructive, I ask teachers on my courses to engage in a writing activity and some collaborative marking (see the INSET ideas at the end of this chapter). The experience is always illuminating for teachers. To begin with, they usually experience some form of anxiety about being judged by a peer, and things like who reads the work first and holding eye contact are highly significant to them. Body language and tone of voice become areas of sensitivity and the importance of receiving some positive comments first are highlighted.

Table 6.1 shows which aspects of body language and verbal language were identified by the participants of one course as having either a positive or a negative impact on them while they were engaged in the process of paired marking.

As a result of various sessions of this kind, the following ground-rules are suggested when embarking on paired marking:

Ground-rules for paired marking

1 Both partners should be roughly the same ability, or just one jump ahead or behind, rather than a wide gap.

2 The student needs time to reflect on and check his or her work before a response partner sees it.

3 The response partner should begin with a positive comment about the work.

Table 6.1

Body language of the response partner:		Verbal language of the response partner:	
Positive	Negative	Positive	Negative
Moving in to look at the work and out when the partner was talking	Avoiding eye contact	Praise	Silences could be positive if encouraging the author to speak, or negative if waiting for the response partner to 'pass judgement'
Smiling	No smiling	Appropriate laughter	No appreciation
Nodding	Foot tapping	Clarification questions	Jumping to conclusions
Holding eye contact	Playing with pens	Empathy over the task	Clipped approach
Hand waving when making a point	Sitting on hands	Reassuring words used	
Facing and mirroring		References to the criteria of the task	
Looking intently at the work			
Pointing to the work			

4   The response partner needs time to take in the student's work, so it is best for the author to read the work out first. This also establishes ownership of the piece.

5   Students need to be trained in the success and improvement process, or whatever is being used, so that they are confident with the steps involved.

6   Students must both agree the part to be changed.

7   The response partner should ask for clarification rather than jump to conclusions.

Carolyn Lyndsay, from St Elizabeth School in Tower Hamlets, explains now how her feedback moved towards self- and paired marking and includes illustrative students' views. I have also included here (Fig. 6.8) her poster of the rules agreed by the class about marking.

Fig. 6.8

'On Tuesday we started to self-mark our own work. I think this is great, I was able to show everyone what was good and how I improved my work. I think sometimes it might be a good leave the response to the next day. You see things you hadn't before. But sometimes you need to do it then, it sort of depends.'

'. . . at first I didn't mind highlighting Charlotte's work, but I didn't want to suggest how she could make it better. I really like Charlotte, and want to be her friend, but then Charlotte said I hadn't told her how to improve. We talked together and worked on a question for her to respond to. I think this was good so that next time I sort of know what to do and if I'm stuck I can just ask them to work with me . . .'

This has frequently been the case . . . I have found that, by introducing self-marking first, students have a structure and process they can fall back on when they move on to paired marking.

'I know that place value is important in decimals, but I can't understand what happens after the hundredths. Miss will need to do more on them, because I think I need just a bit more. I'll put it on a post-it so that she can do something about it.'

I have a system that, as well as circle time, where we raise issues, we also have a post-it board where children can jot down issues and requests . . . we then collectively decide who has to deal with them . . . them, me, us, other adults, school council, parents reps, whoever – hence Rosie's post-it plea.

'I enjoyed helping Kieron on Wednesday. But we didn't agree on the second highlight, so we had to go back to the learning intention and success criteria and really work on them . . . I didn't think they were very good. There was too much in them. Me and Kieron decided on a bit of the learning intention. He said it was the bit he wasn't good at and we then used that for the 'closing the gap' question. I helped him with that. He then looked at mine and it surprised me the bit he asked me to improve, but that's because he was seeing it from the outside, I think that was good.'

(continued)

'I'm still not sure after I have done the first part of the sum if I need to round my answer up or down if it's a word question. I need to get help with this.'

'I knew there was something about my second paragraph in the History so I got Adebola to work with me. Adebola said she couldn't understand it so she asked me to show her the planning and we went to the second paragraph. She asked me to write three bullet points under the heading, then to write a sentence about each bullet point. This was a good idea and I was able to use some of my sentences from the paragraph. I think the report is much better now.'

'Sam's comment in the Spelling Log gave me a new way of remembering those types of words . . . so I gave him one of my ways.'

Our Agreement on Marking Partnerships

We decided that there were some rules we all needed to keep. When we become Marking Partners we all agree to . . .

- **respect** our partner's work because they have done their best and so their work should be valued.

- **try to see** how they have tackled the Learning Intention and only try to improve things that are to do with the learning intention.

- **tell** our partner the good things we see in their work.

- **listen** to our partner's advice because we are trying to help each other do better in our work.

- **look for** a way to help our partner to achieve the Learning Intention better by giving them a 'closing the gap' activity to do.

- try to make our suggestion as **clear** as possible.

- try to make our suggestions **positive**.

- get our partner to **talk about** what they tried to achieve in their work.

- **be fair** to our partner. We will not talk about their work behind their backs because we wouldn't like them to do it to us and it wouldn't be fair.

Fig. 6.9

Photosynthesis

You have been asked to explain to the rest of the people in your group what photosynthesis actually is.

You should be able to tell people where it happens in a plant, what a plant needs to photosynthesise, what is produced, etc.
You should use the equation for photosynthesis too.

Starch test

You have been asked to explain to the rest of the people in your group how to test a leaf for starch.

You should be able to say what you do, and why.
You should also be able to say why plants have starch in their leaves - where it comes from - and what they do with it.

Flowers

You have been asked to explain to the rest of the people in your group about the parts of a flower.

You should be able to name the parts of the flower, and say what each part does to help the plant to reproduce.
You also need to make it clear which pieces are male or female.

Wind and insect pollination

You have been asked to explain to the rest of the people in your group the ways in which flowers are different from wind and insect pollinated plants.

You should be able to describe how and why wind-pollinated plants are different from each other, and to name some examples of each type of plant.

Pollination

You have been asked to explain to the rest of the people in your group exactly what happens when an insect-pollinated flower reproduces.

You should be able to describe where the pollen goes from and to, and how pollination ends up with the formation of a seed.

Seed dispersal and germination

You have been asked to explain to the rest of the people in your group how seeds are spread, and why, and how seeds germinate.

You should be able to explain what a seed is like, what it needs to start to germinate, and why seeds do not need sunlight during germination.

Examples of enabling peer assessment

(a) Assessing explanation

Dave Tuffin and Paul Spencely, from the science department of the Hundred of Hoo School, use traffic-lighting successfully for peer assessment, focusing on students rating each other's explanations of their science knowledge. These teachers developed the following system for use at the end of a unit of work, which results in student self- and peer assessment, revision targets and teacher assessment:

Peer assessment strategy (told by Dave Tuffin)

Introduction
Having completed a section of work, usually a module, lasting approximately six weeks at Key Stage 3, instead of simply asking students to revise for their unit test, I often use a lesson to do group discussion work. This allows me to assess some – although not all – students, and more importantly, it gives the students an opportunity to self-assess and helps them to realise that they need to revise, or work at certain sections.

Brief summary
The activity involves the following:

- Each student, in a group of five or six, explaining a given part of a recent topic to the remainder of the group.

- All students assessing the talks they hear, in relation to their own confidence in the area.

- Students explaining to each other the areas of strength and weakness identified in each other's talks.

Preparation
In advance of the day, I prepare packs of five or six cards, each of which covers a major part of the recently finished topic (see Fig. 6.9 for examples). The cards are distributed – usually at random – amongst a group of students, and each card outlines what the student has to explain to the rest of the group. Depending on the situation and ability, the student has to be given an amount of time with their books to help them prepare. On other occasions, these lessons have followed nominal 'revision' homework, so little, if any time may be allocated for preparation.

The talks
Each student talks for a few minutes, trying to explain his or her given topic in as much detail to the rest of the group as possible. I encourage other students in the group to ask

---

(continued)

any relevant questions, or to have things explained more fully, if they feel that things are not being adequately covered.

Peer and self-assessment

On completion of each talk, the other students 'score' the talk, in private, using a traffic-light system to compare the talk with how they feel they, themselves, could have explained the same topic:

Green – meaning better than I could have done myself.
Amber – meaning about as well as I could have explained it.
Red – meaning not as well as I could have explained this.

Strengths and weaknesses

When all the talks in the group are completed, each student in turn then has their 'scores' revealed. At this stage, if any student has awarded a red or green to somebody, they have to explain to the speaker what they thought was particularly good or particularly poor about the talk.

It is here that students are found to be not only very honest, but are able to discover their own strengths and weaknesses – and not just from the talker. It may be other students who raise items that have been forgotten.

The benefits

I am only able to listen to some talks, and I am careful to target students who I wish to assess for one reason or another – especially helpful for those who do not like to speak in front of the whole class. But it is during the explanations for the 'scores' that I find out most information, and so too do the students. I usually find that it is not necessary to tell students to revise for their upcoming test, as they, themselves, have discovered not only how much is needed, but in which areas time should be targeted.

I am also able to find out which of the five or six main parts of the unit seem to be causing most problem overall, and if there are any general areas of weakness occurring in several groups. *'I thought I knew it all until I tried to explain it to the others, then I realised I didn't'*, is my all-time favourite quote from these lessons.

(b) Peer marking

Spenceley also gives students opportunities to mark each other's work at beginnings of lessons, using the following prompts:

Write two sentences on your partner's work:
Sentence 1: *whether all the info had been included in the work;*
Sentence 2: *how easy it would be to revise from this work.*

Through swapping work around, it is useful to extend this to several students writing their comments on the same work. The work is returned to their owners, who read the comments, then write their own self-assessment, based on the same criteria.

The teacher's comments then build on what has already been written (e.g. *'I agree with xxxx that your work is easy to revise from, but disagree with yyyy that you covered all the info. I feel that you have not adequately explained why terminally ill patients have to take heroin.'*) See Figures 6.10 and 6.11 for students' comments to each other and then Spenceley's responses. Figures 6.12 and 6.13 are further examples of peer-marked work. Fig. 6.14 shows a peer assessment template created by Sally Fisher.

OFSTED (2003) provide another example of effective peer marking:

' *A 35-minute mathematics lesson began smartly with the whole class brainstorming all the statistical terms they had in their jotters, with a description offered for each.*

In turn, three students demonstrated their methods for calculating the mean, mode and range for grouped data, responding confidently to questions raised by members of the class. Students were then asked to work with their 'marking partner' to mark each other's work. The peer marker was asked to consider the following questions:

'Are all the necessary terms included? Do the definitions make sense? Does the explanation of how to calculate the mean, mode and range make sense? Is it complete? Are examples used well to help the explanation? What advice would you give to your partner to improve the draft?'

During the last few minutes the teacher used questions directed at individuals to draw out the main issues and omissions before giving the students three or four minutes to note any alterations they wished to make to their draft. '

Fig. 6.10 Learning objective: To present a balanced factual report (the importance of crude oil and the environmental hazards)

Zoe,

It was really easy to understand.
It was clear what you was trying to
get across. It contains useful facts
about the sea empress and good
figure, about the amount of wildlife
killed or injured.
It contains lots of information and
I think it is really well written.
The only thing you are missing is
a few diagrams, although you
did & such a good report diagrams were
not needed as much.
You have created a good balanced
argument too, you mention the bad
points of crude oil, like environment,
and good points, what we get from
refined crude oil.

like I said before, the only target
you need to think about is including
diagrams.
            Well done Zoe. 😊

    X   Laura-Louise. X

    Thanks, Next time I will
try to include diagrams.
This is an accurate and easy to read report on
crude oil and its uses and effects. I agree with
Laura's comments. You have produced a factual
but well balanced account.   Well done!

Fig. 6.11

I have broken it Down in 5 Sections

1) a good use of information and a good digram for The point you putacross.

2) The Story was soo but ifcarsued a few gustion'S but is really cwser The gustion, you were puting across

3) good use of infor on how The oil Slicke gets worse.

4) good use on who and what gets effectad

5) excelent info on how Thy tryed to get ridof it and Sucseds

B.Coldloe   very good presantion

I understand what you mean on 2). I think I should have worked harder than that.
Thanks for breaking up the project into 5 sections.
I think my diagrams was better than yours.
I think your introduction was better than mine.
Thankyou for a good mark CHEERS!
            rmacoer

(continued)

Nikki - I find Ben's comments very useful on the whole. What aspects of crude oil pollution you did cover were successful and met some of the lesson's objectives about the effects of the oil on the environment. I don't feel that you did enough to balance the argument and explain why crude oil is so important to humans and why, for the time being at least, such oil spillages are likely to continue. Thanks for your effort.

Fig. 6.12 Learning objective: To draw conclusions consistent with the data (electronically controlled robots)

Antony and I found as we increased the voltage the time taken for the robot to travel 2 metres increased. There was a steady increase, and I think if we were to repeat this investigation we would get roughly the same results and patterns. However if I was going to repeat the investigation I would want to control the variables more. The timer should really be activated when the robot starts moving perhaps by a sensor, this would make the results more accurate. We could also have a sensor which switches the timer off. Another thing we noticed was as the investigation went on the wheels picked up dirt and this could have affected the robots performance (also it could have increase friction) If I was repeating this I would try to deal with these things making the test fairer.

Left margin annotation (top): average results and they increase steadily and is mean. You need to discuss this and your results for each voltage, look at your table.

Left margin annotation (bottom): Luke, you have observed the mean average results, but if you look at a wide range voltage have quite the best way of drawing a conclusion.

(continued)

Overall the results show an increase in speed when the voltage is increased. However the decrease in number of seconds taken for the buggy to travel 2 metres is very sharp between 1.5v and 3.0v. The 1.5 result does not seem to follow the pattern of the other results. Although the overall averages (mean) for each voltage indicate a steady increase in speed, the actual trials for 1.5volts have a wide range so I don't really feel that the mean average really indicates the real results. The trials for 1.5V gave data, which didn't follow the pattern. The other trials had results, which only had a range of 2 seconds, however the trials for 1.5V had a range of 6 seconds. I have drawn a graph to show this.

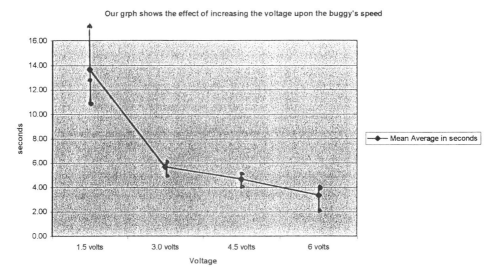

Our grph shows the effect of increasing the voltage upon the buggy's speed

The range does show an increase, but I need to investigate the range of results. I think I need to consider why I got the range – are they accurate result – were there extra variables we had not controlled – did we not control the variables we identified?
Also, I think next time we need to think about the way we display the data and how we use the trials. I mean, is mean the best average or would mode or median be? If we were going to use mode and median, we would have to do many more trials.

(continued)

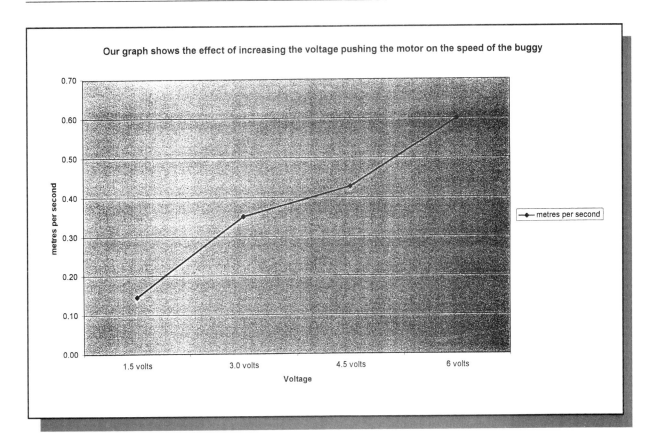

Our graph shows the effect of increasing the voltage pushing the motor on the speed of the buggy

Fig. 6.13 Learning objective: To produce an effective persuasive pamphlet (promoting the Romans)

5. A wood trader who can get to London easily now because on the new roads. Thats good because people can get across easily because of the Romans.

6. A woman living in a Roman town who can buy a wide variety of goods which have come from all over the Roman empire. Thats good because they have sent goods to the shops.

Pamphlet : Assessment of Progress
Comment/Target

X	1	2	3	4	5

well done! you have en included four places to visit and you have organised and underlined your headings Also well done for et including apartments to neat! Next time you need to use adverts to enhance your pamphlet and to include quotes from satisfied customers.

Fig.6.14 Peer assessment template

Peer Assessment Task

You did these really well :

1.

2.

You could have

1.

2.

Next time you need to focus on

1.

2.

Overview: incorporating self- and peer assessment into lessons

Convincing teachers to integrate self- and peer assessment, as in the examples given, is often difficult. When coverage is daunting, these aspects can be seen as other things to fit into the already limited time in a lesson. The important leap is when teachers see self- and peer assessment as unique and highly valuable learning times, which result in students remembering more and having deeper understanding. Many teachers who have been using formative assessment for some time talk about the integration of what used to be ends of lessons or work marked away from the student into the actual structure of a lesson. Time is built-in for reflection in structured ways, as in the examples given in this chapter.

Key principles

- Aim for students constructively marking their own work against the learning objective of the task, sometimes with a partner.

- Students need to be trained, in stages, to mark their own and each other's work.

- There need to be ground rules about paired marking to avoid anxiety.

- Success criteria should be a focus of self-assessment, mainly as a checklist and to identify any help needed.

- Traffic lights are best used with knowledge statements for self-assessment, but can be used successfully in other areas.

- Students can peer-assess their work with a variety of templates and formats.

INSET ideas

1. Share ideas about existing practice for self- and paired marking.
2. Build on this by asking teachers to ask students to find their own successes. Bring examples to a staff meeting and discuss findings.
3. Teachers can trial: students discussing their successes first, then the next stages outlined in this chapter, until students gradually have more control.
4. Set up a staff meeting in which teachers write for four minutes about, say, their journey to school that morning, using a learning objective such as *'Use similes and/or metaphors to add interest and humour to an account.'* They then get into groups of three:

   Two teachers mark one of their pieces together while the third person observes silently, writing under the column headings shown on page 121. They then move round one space, so that, after three goes, each person will have had their work marked cooperatively and each person will have been an observer. They each share their observation findings *at the end*. Ask each group to feed back to the whole staff their findings and recommendations for 'ground-rules' for paired marking.
5. Share ways of using success criteria for self-assessment.
6. Critically discuss the use of traffic lights with reference to the section in this chapter.
7. Trial some of the specific ideas for self- and peer assessment outlined here and feed back findings.

7 Monitoring

‘ *Essentially it is the schools themselves that have it within their control to make substantial impact upon levels of achievement. Schools do not improve simply because of new legislation and because of LEA policy. They do not improve simply because an inspector or an advisory teacher comes to call.* ,

(Craft, 1996)

Monitoring in schools is a key issue for ensuring consistency, continuity and that the rhetoric matches the reality. However, monitoring has associated time-management problems and, if set up inappropriately, can *determine* practice rather than monitor it. For example, it can be tempting to create on paper systems that are easy to monitor, but which would be more effective if they were formatted differently. Getting the *teaching* and *learning* right should be the first priority, then how to *monitor* it the next.

This chapter covers two broad aspects of monitoring: *what* should be monitored, and *how* it should be monitored. Of course, monitoring itself is of no use unless the monitoring information is used and followed up, improving or maintaining the current situation, so this will also be dealt with. Key features of this chapter will be elements of formative assessment.

What assessment should be happening in the school?

Fig. 7.1 is a comprehensive account of the annual cycle of assessment (both formative and summative) for secondary schools, compiled by members of the East Anglia AAIA region. This publication, *Guidelines for Secondary Assessment Coordinators*, is highly recommended (see www.aaia.org.uk).

Fig. 7.1 The annual cycle of assessment

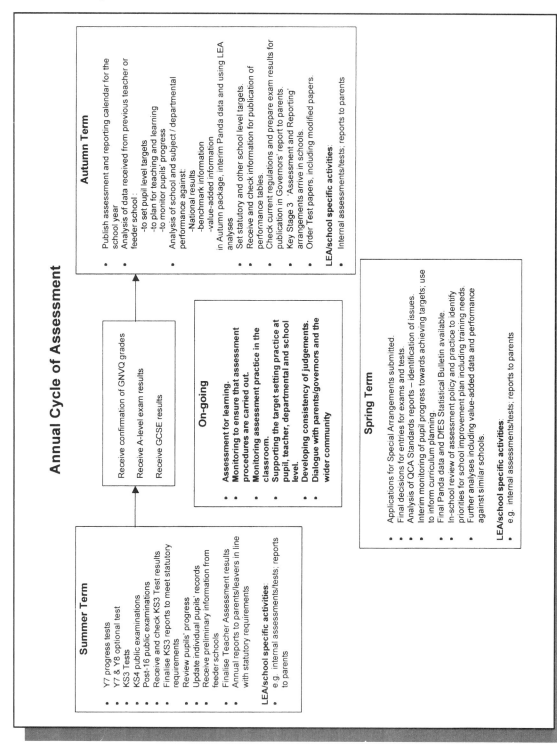

What should be monitored?

The core areas for monitoring are:

- **The curriculum**
  ensuring coverage, continuity and progression, use of resources, quality of learning.

- **Teaching**
  effectiveness in ensuring learning, classroom organisation, class control, etc.

- **Students' progress**
  day-to-day, year-on-year, equal opportunities.

- **Teacher development**
  identifying strengths and weaknesses and finding strategies for development (e.g. management, subject, general, personal).

The QCA (1999) document *Target Setting and Assessment in the National Literacy Strategy* includes the following list, illustrating the various audiences of monitoring:

The class teacher wants to know:

- Has the class overall learned what I planned?

- Are all the students making progress?

- Are they making sufficient progress against national expectations?

- Which individuals need more help in which areas?

- Which students need extension work?

- Is my planning for activities, resources and staffing well targeted?

- How can I do it better next time?

The headteacher and other teachers want to know:

- Are the students making progress?

- Are there any major problems?

- How does their performance compare with those in parallel classes or in other years?

- Is the students' progress in line with the school's targets?
- How is the school doing in comparison with other schools?
- What aspects of our curriculum and teaching need to be strengthened?

The parents/carers want to know:

- Is my student making good progress?
- Are there any major problems?
- How is my student doing compared with others of the same age?
- What can I do to help?

The LEA and national government want to know:

- How is the school and LEA progressing against their targets?
- Are the school development plans working?
- What national curriculum levels are students achieving in teacher assessment and tests?
- How is the school doing in comparison with other similar schools?
- Are the priorities of the LEA's Education Development Plan being met?'

I would like to add another element to this list: the student.

The student wants to know:

- Am I making appropriate progress?
- Is there anything I need to do to improve my progress?
- Are my individual needs being catered for?
- Do I get the chance to use different learning styles?
- Do I have a chance to be self-evaluative and have those thoughts been taken account of?

How should it be monitored?

A good starting-point is to consider the possible monitoring mechanisms. These form a menu, which establishes the backbone of a monitoring framework. We then need to consider the various advantages and disadvantages of each mechanism and decide which are most effective.

Possible monitoring mechanisms

Formal strategies (time needed)

1. Work sampling
2. Classroom observations
3. Target sampling
4. Job profiling/teacher appraisal/performance management
5. Discussion between Assessment Coordinator and Head of Department
6. Discussion between Head of Department and subject teacher
7. Analysis of test data
8. Tracking of numerical targets
9. Analysis of LEA comparative data
10. Analysis of national comparative data
11. Analysis of medium-term plans
12. Analysis of short-term plans
13. Analysis of school reports
14. Looking through students' work

Informal, incidental or externally based strategies

15. Student feedback
16. Parent feedback
17. Governor feedback
18. Staff meeting feedback
19. Informal exchanges between staff (before and after school, etc)

20. SENCO perspective

21. External perspective (e.g. inspectors)

In deciding on regular formal monitoring mechanisms, it is important to select strategies which are most time-effective. Teachers tend to find that it is more effective to have a longer, richer, but less frequent monitoring time than to have many discrete monitoring activities taking place across the school. For example, taking in samples of students' work across a year group or school for scrutiny by curriculum coordinators is often a superficial exercise. Without the teacher present, and the corresponding weekly plan, sampled work can have too many missing factors for any worthwhile or rigorous judgement to be made. *Combining* monitoring mechanisms (see 1, 2 and 3 above) makes monitoring more satisfying and effective, because the links can be made between planning, subsequent learning, work products and targets.

Who monitors what?

Figures 7.2 and 7.3 define roles for monitoring assessment in the secondary school (East Anglia AAIA region publication).

Effective observations

As *observation* is the most powerful mechanism for effective monitoring, some detail now follows.

Conditions for successful observation

In order to make classroom observations manageable and worthwhile, we need to look at conditions for success, how time can be found, and how observations can be followed up. The following lists are drawn from research about monitoring as well as feedback from heads and teachers.

- There needs to be a whole-school policy and structure for observations.

- Planning needs to be clear and tight to enable monitoring to have a starting point (i.e. what is the learning objective and the matched activity?).

Fig. 7.2 Who does what?

Who Does What?

Head Teacher & Senior Management

Head Teachers and their Leadership Teams have a duty to ensure that the school
meets statutory requirements in relation to assessment, including the setting of targets.
They will also evaluate the impact of assessment on raising standards within the school.
The Head Teacher will need to define the roles of assessment co-ordinators and others
involved in assessment and disseminate relevant information to them.

Structures within schools will vary, but all teachers are likely to be key contributors to quality
assessment and target setting processes. However, the following staff are crucial to effective
assessment procedures.

Assessment Co-ordinator

The Assessment co-ordinator has the key role in the analysis and interpretation of
performance data and in developing effective assessment practice across the school.
To achieve this the co-ordinator should:

- Prepare and publish a timetable of events associated with the assessment cycle
- Lead on development and review of whole school assessment policy including
  marking
- Identify assessment priorities for school improvement plan
- Identify and support training needs
- Ensure assessment systems are manageable and that assessment data is
  effectively gathered and collated
- Disseminate assessment information throughout the school
- Analyse assessment data (from feeder schools, NC Tests, GCSE, GNVQ, GCE etc)
  to monitor school effectiveness and inform setting of targets
- Support colleagues in using assessment information/data including the Autumn
  package
- Ensure that statutory requirements are met
- Check that subject department assessment policies are in line with school policy,
  are up to date and regularly reviewed
- Support subject leaders in ensuring that schemes of work identify appropriate
  assessment opportunities
- Link with subject leaders to ensure coherence of pupil experience across the
  curriculum
- Check subject departments carry out procedures to agree standards and generate
  portfolios of moderated work
- Consult with subject leaders/heads of year etc. to ensure subject assessment data is
  made available as required
- Prepare data for governors' report to parents

(continued)

Who Does What?

Subject Leader

- Develop an assessment policy for the subject in line with school policy.
- Ensure schemes of work include clear learning objectives and a range of strategies for assessment within the subject.
- Ensure the focus within the classroom is upon assessment for learning.
- Check that assessment and marking procedures are implemented effectively
- Develop consistency of judgements through agreement of standards and generating portfolios of moderated pupils' work.
- Analyse and interpret data with the subject team to monitor standards and set appropriately challenging targets .
- Use data to review the curriculum with the subject team
- Ensure progress towards targets is regularly monitored.
- Report to SMT and Governors on standards .

Subject Teacher

- Implement assessment **for** learning within the classroom
- Enable pupils to develop the skills of self-assessment
- Identify pupils in need of support. Liaise with SENCO (IEP)
- Use agreed range of assessment methods and techniques to gather and use information in line with school's policies
- Record significant progress
- Review evidence and finalise Teacher Assessment
- Implement school based and/or national statutory tests/tasks
- Contribute to departmental discussion on performance data.
- Report to parents – pupil progress, attainment, next steps
- Ensure information is available for next teacher or school.

EMTAG

The EMTAG Co-ordinator will have particular responsibility for monitoring and assessing the performance of ethnic minority pupils and setting them challenging targets. In addition they will be working collaboratively with teachers to ensure full access to the curriculum through planning and teaching.

SENCO

- In liaison with other staff, identify pupils with SEN and assess their specific needs
- Work with other staff to develop and support appropriate assessment methods and differentiation for pupils on the SEN Register
- Liaise with external agencies over formal assessment for statementing
- Monitor and evaluate performance data for pupils on the Register
- Arrange appropriate adaptations to end of Key Stage assessments.

Fig. 7.3

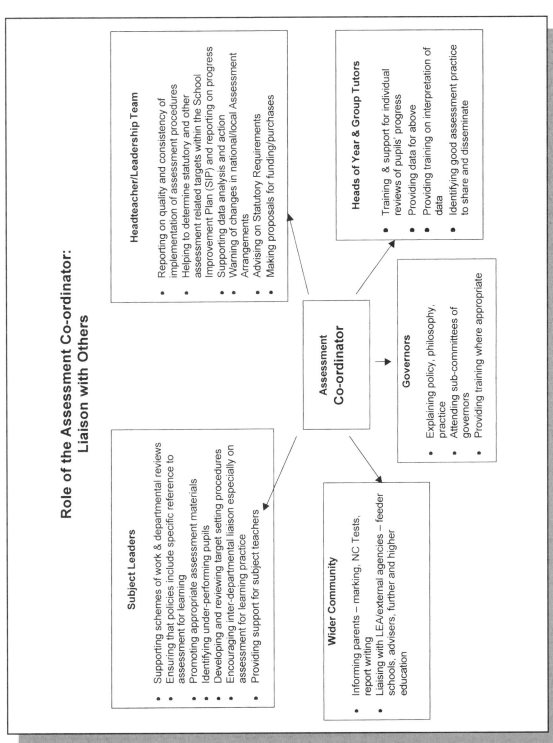

Role of the Assessment Co-ordinator: Liaison with Others

Headteacher/Leadership Team
- Reporting on quality and consistency of implementation of assessment procedures
- Helping to determine statutory and other assessment related targets within the School Improvement Plan (SIP) and reporting on progress
- Supporting data analysis and action
- Warning of changes in national/local Assessment Arrangements
- Advising on Statutory Requirements
- Making proposals for funding/purchases

Heads of Year & Group Tutors
- Training & support for individual reviews of pupils' progress
- Providing data for above
- Providing training on interpretation of data
- Identifying good assessment practice to share and disseminate

Assessment Co-ordinator

Governors
- Explaining policy, philosophy, practice
- Attending sub-committees of governors
- Providing training where appropriate

Subject Leaders
- Supporting schemes of work & departmental reviews
- Ensuring that policies include specific reference to assessment for learning
- Promoting appropriate assessment materials
- Identifying under-performing pupils
- Developing and reviewing target setting procedures
- Encouraging inter-departmental liaison especially on assessment for learning practice
- Providing support for subject teachers

Wider Community
- Informing parents – marking, NC Tests, report writing
- Liaising with LEA/external agencies – feeder schools, advisers, further and higher education

- Observer and teacher need to agree the focus, terms and nature of what is to be observed.

- Only key points should be recorded by the observer.

- Short feedback should follow on the same day.

- The observer should make a few positive points, then ask the teacher how the session went.

- The observer should sum up discussion and offer suggestions.

- Both should keep a copy of the final summary and action, for follow-up use.

Of key importance when carrying out classroom observations is that the *criteria* for observation are written and given to the person being observed, so that both observer and observee are aware of the aspects being judged. Without this knowledge, the teacher is cast in the role of the student who does not know the learning objective of a task. Too many criteria can make the observer spend the entire time trying to keep track of them, and much of a lesson can be missed by the observer writing furiously. It is better to have a few, focused criteria. Whatever the subject of the person observing, formative assessment will be embedded in the practice of a school if there are always some generic assessment criteria listed for observations.

The following list simply turns the various formative assessment strategies into observation criteria:

Generic assessment criteria for observations

1. Is the learning objective clearly shown in the short-term plan?

2. Is there a match between learning objective and task?

3. Is the learning objective shared explicitly with students, both orally and visually, at the beginning of the session?

4. Is the learning objective the focus of oral feedback and/or written marking during the session?

5. Are questions worthwhile: do they explore issues that are critical to the development of students' understanding?

6. Are there opportunities for students to discuss questions asked or to work together during the course of the lesson?

7. Is there some opportunity for students to engage in self- or peer evaluation or reflection?

How are observations followed up?

- Feed back to teacher at once, using a simple proforma to record action.

- Follow up at next observation.

- Follow up at job profiling/appraisal meeting.

If teachers feel threatened by classroom observations, the following aspects can help build a monitoring culture. However, monitoring will only be considered worthwhile by teachers if they can see the positive effects and follow-up for the students and/or the school, or in their own personal development.

Creating an observation/monitoring culture

- Make observation commonplace:
  - Head of Department monitoring first;
  - getting inspectors to observe;
  - organise pairs of teachers to observe in other schools.

- Introduce job profiling, which links with observations.

- Ensure observation rules are established – especially the focus and criteria.

- Ensure that subject coordinators are sufficiently expert to be able to give advice.

- Ensure teaching is underpinned by effective planning procedures.

The teacher's perspective

An assessment coordinator's story, taken from the AAIA booklet *Secondary Practice: Self-Evaluation and Development Materials*, gives a reality check to the challenge of monitoring:

'   *"We are successful because we practise what we are not good at."* These words, attributed to the New Zealand "All Blacks" rugby captain during a period of world domination in the sport, have stuck in *my mind. He claimed that too often we spent time embellishing what we are already good at doing. To be truly successful, teams need to identify their areas of weakness and work at these, however difficult.*

An assessment coordinator for four years now, I see value in this observation. I asked a group of my colleagues to tell me of their least favourite teaching module coming up in the next few weeks. "Chaucer . . . sheep farming . . . chemical equations . . ." and so on. We agreed that, in our least favourite teaching tasks, we were almost going through the motions to satisfy the scheme of work. Learning outcomes were woollier than the sheep themselves. Two other significant points were made. First, did we always know the areas where we thought we taught effectively and where students made progress in their learning? Secondly, did we know which colleagues really did know how to teach an understanding of a chemical equation effectively?

We are now spending much more time as subject teams, analysing the learning outcomes of module tests and activities, making ourselves identify "what we are (not) good at", chiefly as a department, but also perhaps as a school. We are paying far closer attention to GCSE subject reports, KS3 national analysis and to LEA advisor comment. We have tried to nominate a colleague for each subject whose job it is to relate our findings, with national and local observations. We know that time for such research is limited and barely scientific. However, by focusing as a team on areas which we have found to have weaker learning outcomes for students – or where we have admitted to personal lack of confidence – we are getting a more even, consistent quality into our subject teaching. ❟

(AAIA, 2003)

Key principles

- Teaching and learning principles and practice come first: how to monitor them second.

- Make sure easy monitoring procedures don't dictate practice.

- Monitoring information must be used to be useful.

- Aim for longer, richer monitoring mechanisms rather than many short, superficial exercises.

- Observation is the most effective vehicle for monitoring, and needs agreed procedures and criteria.

INSET ideas (Head of Department meetings)

1. Audit the school's current monitoring practice, determining the effectiveness of the monitoring strategies in action so far.
2. Introduce the monitoring strategies list and decide what would be really useful for your context.
3. The various elements of monitoring need to be finely tuned: for example, creating simple proformas for observations and criteria lists for classroom observations.
4. Have a staff meeting after the first year to review the effectiveness of the monitoring strategies used in the school's programme of monitoring.
5. Continue the process of review.

8 Using this book to make a difference

> ❝ Since formal education was introduced in this country the emphasis has always been on what we want students to learn . . . now we have realised that it is equally important to look at how students learn . . . putting the two together is little short of a revolution. ❞
>
> *(Broadfoot, 2003)*

The question I am most often asked after training sessions is *'How am I going to take all of this back to school?'* There is no simple answer, but this chapter contains some of the strategies and ways forward that schools have so far found successful. But first, some of the eternal problems associated with effecting change, and some solutions . . .

Effecting change

One of the most daunting aspects of being the assessment coordinator is finding the best ways of effecting change. On my courses, I have asked participants to brainstorm all the things that *can* go wrong. From that, Table 8.1 has been developed: the problem is stated, the reason for the problem discussed and the best strategies for dealing with the problem shared. The list could be much longer, but the strategies here can be applied to many situations where change produces difficulty.

Table 8.1

Problem	Reason	Strategies
Teachers always seeing negative aspects	They want an easy life. They don't feel valued. They feel threatened. Enjoy being the Devil's Advocate. People don't like change and new things.	Be positive. Don't react in a defensive, negative way. Try to raise their self-esteem. Work with the people who are interested in action research and use them for a pilot to be fed back to the rest. Emphasise the fact that formative assessment is about being an **action researcher** – making mistakes, finding it hard at first, taking it slowly, experimenting. Approach the most negative people before the meeting and ask for their advice – take them into your confidence about possible difficulties with staff, etc – they often respond to being involved. Before running a staff meeting on any new element, go to every member of staff over a period of time, discussing it with them personally and asking for their views and advice. By the meeting it is usually a 'fait accompli' or, at least, they are on your side and discussions are conducted professionally.
'I've seen it all before'	They've taught for 25 years the same way. Things do come round and can be depressing.	Need more contact with other schools and teachers who are using formative assessment. **See above**
'It won't work with our kids'	Fear of trying something new with 'difficult' students. Fear of involving such students more actively.	Lead by example! Trial with more challenging classes and feedback to staff. Use samples of formative assessment work carried out by the above classes. Where possible, use real students' names.

Problem	Reason	Strategies
'Tell me what to do'	They don't understand the new ideas. Feel pressurised. Don't want the burden of extra work – too busy.	Give support. Whole school needs to look at areas in more depth. Staff have to be involved in the process. Have more small-group discussions so they have to think for themselves: talking partners.
Negative body language	Not interested. Don't like the person leading the staff meeting. Tired at the end of the day.	Involve the staff in the meeting. Make it active and short. If necessary, the senior management team should confront the person privately and say it is noticeable and is unprofessional and must stop (asking if the person needs support first, etc)
People not being able to say what they think	Dominant personalities, hierarchy.	Carefully select small groups in meetings (e.g. group people by equal status rather than mixed, so all will feel confident to speak)
Dominant personalities	Feel they have high status. Appear secure. Trying to prove they are 'good' teachers.	See above + management of meeting
Falls asleep	Tired, old, pregnant, ill, been out all night, bored.	Vary styles of meeting. Keep windows open, strong black coffee, chocolate for energy. Ground-rules needed.
Viewing new initiatives as more work	Overloaded, asked to do too much.	Trialling periods to know the worth of the project. Prioritising. Provide release to support new initiatives. Arrange feedback meetings about something specific.
No definite decisions are made or are obvious.	Poor management. Meeting rambles so needs more time.	Agenda must itemise. Chair must make statement of what stage has been reached for each item, even if only that the thing will have to be carried over or become a working party or small

Problem	Reason	Strategies
		group discussion. Sometimes decisions can't be made because there needs to be some action to see if it works rather than keep talking hypothetically. Trial and review everything.
They agree but carry on regardless	Know they can. Want a quiet life at meeting but know they can get away with it.	Monitoring issue and feedback meetings needed where everyone must contribute. Reminders sent a few days before.
Staff not airing views at meeting but outside	Intimidated – large groups. Unsure of themselves, inadequate, lack of trust. Not feeling views will be valued, based on past experience. Not fully aware – not taking on board their roles and responsibilities.	Small groups in meetings. Long-term aim to change ethos. Recognise the problem and identify causes (personalities, history). Set out clear role definitions and job descriptions.
Not enough follow-up meetings to ensure change occurs	Poor planning – expecting to achieve too much.	Plan the meetings in advance – make a commitment to formative assessment. In advance, ask for people's written views by a certain date, although it is better to talk to them.
Decisions are made but they are impossible to carry out.	Panic – too much change needed, not knowing where to start. Lack of organisation/ resources. Not delegating, monitoring roles within tasks	Break down into manageable chunks via an action plan. Team needed with clear allocation of responsibility. Feedback to staff – feasibility, manageability. Keep people informed. Feed back to staff on positive achievement.
People who don't ask for help	Lack of confidence, fear of seeming a failure, older staff expect that they should know. NQTs fear of being judged. Demoralisation. Don't know who to ask – think they are too busy.	Monitoring. Structured programme of observation and positive feedback. Clear role and responsibility structure. Senior management check monitoring is working. Mentor in year group for new staff.

Getting started with formative assessment: process success criteria for teachers!

Remember to . . .

■ Get Senior Management Team support

It must be clear that senior managers not only support the introduction of formative assessment, but are committed to seeing it happen, giving time and resource support for extensive trialling and meetings. A new school policy on assessment will need to be drawn up reflecting formative assessment principles. SMT also need to ensure there are systems in place for new staff to be inducted into formative assessment.

■ Take your time

Formative assessment often involves major changes in people's thinking and needs time to be trialled, discussed and created by schools. It would be better to wait two years until there is a serious commitment on the school or departmental development plan to formative assessment, than to try to rush it in a few staff meetings.

■ Decide the best way to start

Some schools prefer to ask a few keen teachers to trial some of the strategies first before embarking on whole school trialling. These teachers not only feed back their work at a later date, but have often by then ironed out practical problems which everyone otherwise would have encountered. Most importantly, their success makes the notion of formative assessment credible and viable for the individual school context. There is often natural curiosity from others about how the action research is going, so the osmosis effect happens naturally at this stage.

> *What is needed is a plan, extending over at least three years, in which a few small groups are supported for a two-year exploration, and they then form a basis of experience and expertise for disseminating within the school and supporting their colleagues in making similar explorations for themselves.*

(Black et al., 2002)

■ Base decisions on research principles

The Key Principles given at the end of each chapter list the things that really matter. When deciding on ways of working, take account of these principles rather than the practical strategies. If the strategies are trialled without the underlying principle being understood, teachers can use them superficially. It is better to present the research in each case and first ask teachers what they believe are already doing to fulfil those principles. The ideas in this book can then be given as some possible things to trial.

■ Build on existing practice

Formative assessment is not another initiative: it is about teachers being **action researchers**, continually finding better ways of helping students to learn. Any practical strategies outlined in this book are derived from teachers, and each should be seen as another suggestion adding to the teacher's existing repertoire, rather than to replace it.

Teachers need to be encouraged to be action researchers trialling not only ideas from this book but their own ideas. There will be successes and failures, and students and staff need time to grow into new ways of working and thinking, so they need to be encouraged not to give up! The end result should be modified strategies, which schools and teachers have created for themselves, using books like this, and the other resources referenced here, as a resource.

■ Keep a journal

It is a good idea to encourage teachers to keep a 'learning journal' in which they jot their ideas, make notes on successful lessons, quotes from students and so on. This keeps the focus on formative assessment and equips teachers with specific anecdotes for departmental or other staff meetings. Too often, teachers forget the details of spectacular lessons and can only speak in generalities. The specifics allow other teachers to see clearly what happened and how it impacted on student learning, making their own application more feasible.

■ Share findings

Teachers say it takes at least two years to embed, and that is with lots of staff meetings and informal staff discussions. Ideally you should introduce aspects of formative assessment one at a time, allowing input, discussion and feedback staff meetings. On my training days, I input for half the time and get people to try things out in the other half. Sharing and analysing people's attempts at creating success criteria or making improvement prompts, for instance, really moves people in their understanding. After two or three meetings like this, people feel much more confident in planning or implementing new elements of their practice alone.

■ Don't go it alone

Get teachers to observe each other and work closely together wherever possible. Observing each other teach, with a clear focus, is highly productive if there is mutual trust and respect.

Grab any opportunity to form a network of schools in which the same element is being explored, so that teachers can be observed and strategies and findings can be shared. Visit my website (www.shirleyclarke-education.org) for regular updates on the findings of the various Learning Teams around the country.

■ Involve students

Ask students for their opinions about the strategies throughout. Ask for their feelings about particular elements before and then after introducing formative assessment. This will obviously become more fruitful as time progresses and students have had more opportunities to discuss and analyse together and put forward their views more freely.

Creating a School Council is a further indicator to students that they have a say in their education and that their opinions are valued. Students in one school put forward the request that they would like all teachers to know which strategies used across the school by the various teachers were considered most successful in helping them learn. The school was well into formative assessment practices, so it is not surprising that such a confident request was made. Formative assessment allows students to communicate their needs with confidence.

■ Keep it going

Once formative assessment has been introduced, it is important to keep momentum in the following ways:

■ Make sure the strategies are monitored, especially by classroom observation (see Chapter 7).

■ Make the strategies visually obvious throughout the school.

■ Refer to the strategies during whole-school events such as assemblies, so that all staff and students know the common language of achievement.

■ Write an assessment policy, which outlines exactly how formative assessment is carried out, under the headings of the various chapters. Make sure everyone has copies of this.

■ Produce parent-friendly news-sheets along the way, as each strategy is introduced, so that parents are fully informed and encouraged to support their child's new development.

■ Produce summaries of the assessment policy when it is finished, to show all relevant parties.

■ Continue to review the strategies in action, consulting all parties involved – especially students.

Endnote from Shirley

Teachers are rarely told how expert they have become. In my travels around the world I have been struck many times by how far we have come in the last 15 years. UK teachers have exceptional expertise, which is still developing and growing, in their own subjects and in basing learning on learning objectives. They have access to wonderful resources and have considerably elevated their expectations of students.

Feedback from teachers applying formative assessment strategies has been overwhelming. As the research demonstrates, formative assessment makes a significant difference to students' progress – in their ability to be confident, critical learners, to achieve more than ever before and in raising their self-esteem.

What is needed now is high teacher morale, greater power and more professional confidence. The ingredients are all there for teachers to pay more attention to learning than coverage, to focusing on what works best for the learning rather than for accountability and to make lessons fit the *students'* learning needs rather than the needs of outside parties. Hopefully, this book will inspire teachers to grab their professional confidence with both hands.

Endnote from a teacher

 The project has impressed upon me the need to encourage independence in students; too often they expect to be passively "spoon fed" a syllabus, while we succeed not in extending their creativity but in quashing it. By the careful use of questioning, by encouraging students to critically reflect on their own and on others' work and by making them partners in the teaching and learning processes, I believe we can make a real difference for the better.

Katrina Harrell, head of an English Department (in Black et al., 2003)

Endnote from a student

 I transferred here from middle school. Nobody had told me there what to do to improve my work. Now I know exactly how to improve my grades. I know the criteria for particular marks in an assignment, and it's my fault if I don't do the work.

(Phillip, Year 9, quoted in OFSTED, 2003)

References

AAIA (Association of Assessment Inspectors and Advisors) (2001) *Primary Assessment Practice: Evaluation and Development Materials* (www.aaia.org.uk)

AAIA (2003) *Secondary Practice: Self-evaluation and Development Materials* (www.aaia.org.uk)

Abbott, J. (1994) *Learning Makes Sense*, in Education 2000 conference papers.

Assessment Reform Group (1999) *Assessment for Learning: Beyond the Black Box*, University of Cambridge School of Education.

Assessment Reform Group (2002) *Assessment for Learning: Ten Principles* (www.assessment-reform-group.org.uk)

Abrami, P., Chambers, B., Poulsen, C., De Simone, C., Dápollonia, S. and Howden, J. (1995) *Classroom Connections: understanding and using co-operative learning,* Toronto: Harcourt Brace, quoted from Carnell, E. (2000) 'Dialogue, discussion and feedback', in Askew, S. (Ed.) *Feedback for Learning*, RoutledgeFalmer.

Askew, S. and Lodge, C. (2000) 'Gifts, ping-pong and loops-linking feedback and learning', in Askew, S. (Ed.) *Feedback for Learning*, RoutledgeFalmer.

Ausubel, D. P., Novak, J. and Hanesian, H. (1978) *Educational Psychology: A Cognitive View*, 2nd edn, Holt Rinehart and Winston.

BASS (Birmingham Advisory and Support Service) (2003) *Assessment for Learning- a revolution in classroom practice*, VIDEO Bass Publications, Martineau Centre, Balden Road, Harborne, Birmingham B32 2EH (tel. 0121 303 8081).

Black, P. and Wiliam, D. (1998) 'Assessment and classroom learning', *Assessment in Education, 5*, 1.

Black, P. and Wiliam, D. (1998) *Inside the Black Box: Raising Standards through Classroom Assessment*, London: King's College School of Education.

Black, P., Harrison, C., Lee, C., Marshall, B. and Wiliam, D. (2003) *Assessment for Learning*, Open University Press.

Broadfoot, P. (2003) quoted in BASS Assessment For Learning training video (see above)

Brooks, J.G. and Brooks, M.G. (1993) *In Search of Understanding: the case for constructivist classrooms*, Alexandria, VA, Association for Supervision and Curriculum Development.

Butler, R. (1988) 'Enhancing and undermining intrinsic motivation; the effects of task-involving and ego-involving evaluation on interest and performance', *British Journal of Educational Psychology*, 58, 1–14.

Clarke S. website for previous publications and Learning Teams updates: www.shirleyclarke-education.org

Cowie, B. and Bell, B. (1999) 'A model of formative assessment in science education', *Assessment in Education*, 6, 1, 101–16.

Craft, A. (1996) in MacGilchrist, B. (ed.) *Managing Access and Entitlement in Primary Education*, Routledge.

Crooks, T. (2001) Paper prepared for the 2001 Annual Meeting of the British Educational Research Association (BERA), Leeds, England, 13–15 September 2001 (in proceedings, but not presented because of travel delays caused by terrorist actions).

Dahl, R. (1984) *Boy: Tales of Childhood*, Puffin Books, The Penguin Group.

De Bono, E., in Sullivan (2003) *Questions Worth Asking*, The Brighton and Hove Assessment for Learning Project, Brighton and Hove LEA.

DfES (2002) *Teaching and Learning in the Foundation Subjects*, module 4 (Questioning), ref. 0350/2002

Dryden, G. and Vos, J. (2001) *The Learning Revolution*, Network Educational Press.

Dweck, C. (1986) 'Motivational processes affecting learning', *American Psychologist*, *41*, 1041–8.

Elstgeest, J. (1985) 'The right question at the right time', in Harlen, W. (ed.) *Taking the Plunge: how to teach science more effectively*, Heinemann.

Eppig, P. (1981) *Education by Design* – used in the UK as Critical Skills program by Success@Bristol (Bristol Education Action Zone).

Gardner, H., (1983*) Frames of Mind*, Basic Books.

Hargreaves, E., McCallum, B. and Gipps, C. (2001) 'Teacher feedback strategies in primary classrooms-new evidence', in Askew, S. (ed.) *Feedback for Learning*, RoutledgeFalmer.

Hattie, J. (1992) 'Towards a model of schooling: a synthesis of meta-analyses', Australian Journal of Education, *36*, 5–13.

Kluger, A.N. and DeNisi, A. (1996) 'The effects of feedback interventions on performance: a historical review, a meta-analysis, and a preliminary feedback intervention theory', *Psychological Bulletin*, *119*, 2, 258–84.

Knight, S. (2000) *Questions: Assessing and Developing Students's Understanding and Thinking in Literacy*, Manchester School Improvement Service (tel. 0161 610 3333).

OfSTED (2003) *Good Assessment in Secondary Schools* and Key Stage 3 documents: www.dfes.gov.uk

Perkins, D. (1992) *Smart Schools*, Free Press.

Perrenoud, P. (1991) 'Towards a pragmatic approach to formative evaluation', in Weston, P. (ed.) *Assessment of Pupils' Achievement: Motivation and School Success*, Amsterdam: Swets and Zeitlinger.

QCA website: www.qca.org.uk for The LEARN Project and the Assessment for Learning site.

QCA (1999) *Target Setting and Assessment in the National Literacy Strategy*, Qualifications and Curriculum Authority.

Rowe, M. B. (1974) 'Relation of wait-time and rewards to the development of language, logic and fate control', *Journal of Research in Science Teaching*, *11*, 4, 292 (in High Scope, 1995).

Sadler, R. (1989) 'Formative assessment and the design of instructional systems', *Instructional Science*, *18*, 119–44.

Stevenson, H. W. and Stigler, J. W. (1992) *The Learning Gap*, Touchstone/Simon & Schuster.

Stigler, J.W. and Hiebert, J. (1999) *The Teaching Gap*, Free Press/Simon & Schuster.

Suffolk LEA references: www.slamnet.org.uk

Sullivan, [initial?] (2003) *Questions worth asking*, The Brighton and Hove Assessment for Learning Project.

Vispoel, W. P. and Austin, J. R. (1995) 'Success and failure in junior high school: a critical incident approach to understanding students' attributional beliefs', *American Educational Research Journal*, *32*, 2, 377–412.

Vygotsky, L. S. (1978) *Mind in Society*, Harvard University Press.

Weatherley, C. (2000) *Leading the Learning School* (School Effectiveness Series, general series editor: Tim Brighouse), Network Educational Press.

Youngs, B. B. *The Six Vital Ingredients of Self-Esteem: How to develop them in your students,* in Dryden, G. and Boss, J. (op. cit).